MANAGING
NEGOTIATIONS

MANAGING NEGOTIATIONS

THIRD EDITION

GAVIN KENNEDY
JOHN BENSON
JOHN McMILLAN

CENTURY
BUSINESS

Copyright © Gavin Kennedy, John Benson and John McMillan,
1980, 1984, 1987

The rights of Gavin Kennedy, John Benson and John McMillan to
be identified as authors of this work have been asserted by them in
accordance with the Copyright Designs and Patents Act 1988

Buisiness Books Limited
An imprint of Random Century Ltd
20 Vauxhall Bridge Road
London SW1V 2SA

Random Century Australia (Pty) Ltd
20 Alfred Street, Milsons Point, Sydney,
New South Wales 2061, Australia

Random Century New Zealand Ltd
18 Poland Road, Glenfield,
Auckland 10, New Zealand

Random Century South Africa (Pty) Ltd
PO Box 337, Bergvlei 2012, South Africa

First published 1980
Reprinted 1981 (three times), 1982
Second edition 1984
Reprinted 1985, 1986
Third edition 1987
Reprinted 1987, 1988, 1989 (as Better Business Guide), 1990 (twice), 1991

Set in 11 on 12 point Baskerville by
Input Typesetting Ltd., London SW19 8DR

Printed and bound in Great Britain by
Mackays of Chatham PLC, Chatham, Kent

British Library Cataloguing in Publication Data

Kennedy, Gavin
   Managing negotiations.—3rd ed.
   1.Negotiation in business
   I. Title   II. Benson, John, *1945 Sep 6-*
   III. McMillan, John, *1947-*
   658.4'5   HD58.6

ISBN 0-09-168891-4

For our children
Joanne, Vicky, Sarah, Russell, Claire,
Kim, Karen, Florence, Beatrice
and Gavin
the best negotiators of all

Contents

Preface to the Third Edition

The continuing success of Managing Negotiations has necessitated a third edition. Many thousands of managers have read
previous editions, and their comments and suggestions for
improvements have always been welcome, as well as their
generous praise for what we set out to do in 1980 with the
first edition, namely to provide a thoroughly practical book
on the complexities of negotiation.

The Eight-Step Approach was first developed in 1974 by
Gavin Kennedy and John Benson, for a series of negotiating
skills courses run for Scottish & Newcastle Breweries in Edinburgh. It has proven robust in more than 12 years of regular
training programmes run by the authors, and by many other
trainers who have adapted our materials. Interestingly, other
trainers, working quite independently here and abroad, have
developed similar approaches to our's (we know of a 'four
step' and a 'six step' approach, and there is, of course, the
'four phase' approach adapted from Managing Negotiations
for Rank Training's video, The Art of Negotiating, in 1981).

The authors have continued to develop negotiating skills
training in their different career paths. But a lot of help has
also been received from Tony Martin, Richard Rowland,
Robbie Robinson, Stephen White, and Colin Rose and Ian
Heriot (of Rose & Heriot, Mt Macedon, Victoria) in
Australia.

John McMillan, in partnership with Stephen White and
Richard Rowland, has developed Scotwork into a major
training organization both in the UK and worldwide. Scot-

work courses are running almost every week in Glasgow, Coventry and Bournemouth. John spends three months a year running negotiating courses in the United States. In 1986, John McMillan, Stephen White and Gavin Kennedy produced a three day training package — The Scotwork Negotiating Skills Portfolio — for companies wishing to train 50 or more managers using the Eight-Step Approach. Details of the Portfolio, and all Scotwork courses can be obtained from: Scotwork, 7 Fortrose Street, Glasgow, G11 5NU (Telephone: 041–357 3989).

John Benson joined the board of Nabisco in 1984 and continues his career as one of the UK's leading industrial relations and personnel management specialists. He is much in demand for speaking engagements at high level management conferences and at major functions of the Institute of Personnel Management. John Benson has continued his record of innovative approaches to management activities.

Gavin Kennedy was appointed a Professor in the department of Accountancy and Finance, at Heriot–Watt University, Edinburgh, in 1985. He has continued to publish best-selling books on negotiation: Everything is Negotiable, (1983), Negotiate Anywhere, (1985), Superdeal, (1986), which have been translated into Dutch, Swedish, Spanish, and 'American'. In 1986 he produced 'Negotiating Skills', a video–book training package from Guild Sound and Vision Ltd for companies and individuals. He is Managing Director of Negotiate Ltd, consultant negotiators and trainers, and runs senior Negotiating Clinics in the UK, Scandanavia, North America and Australia. Negotiate Ltd can be contacted at 22 Braid Avenue, Edinburgh, EH10 6EE (Telephone: 031–452 8404, Telex 72165 or Fax: 031–452 8388).

Edinburgh, Reading and Glasgow 1986   GAVIN KENNEDY
                                             JOHN BENSON
                                             JOHN McMILLAN

Preface to the Second Edition

In 1981 Rank made a training film based on the Eight-Step Approach (*The Art of Negotiating*) which has been a successful venture for all concerned. They found it impossible to fit eight steps into a 30-minute film without overpowering the viewer with detail, and settled for a Four-Phase Approach (PREPARE, DISCUSS, PROPOSE and BARGAIN), with subordinate references to the signal, package, close and agree steps.

We have no quarrel with this adaptation. Our Eight-Step Approach has always been seen as a training and working tool to be used as suits the individual and the circumstances, rather than as a strait-jacket. We decided not to alter the second edition to reflect the line of the training film, believing that the Eight-Step Approach has a contribution to make to the understanding of, and participation in, negotiations in all walks of life, and that the four-phase version supports rather than contradicts our method.

Edinburgh, Reading and Glasgow 1984   GAVIN KENNEDY
                                             JOHN BENSON
                                             JOHN McMILLAN

Preface to the First Edition

Managing Negotiations arose from the fruitful collaboration of the authors in running training courses for managers in negotiation skills. But many others contributed to the book by virtue of their contribution to the training courses as tutors or participants (the distinction has never been insisted upon nor has it always been obvious).

The book has been jointly written by the authors, blending our experience both as practitioners and trainers. It is thoroughly practical in outlook and does not refer the reader to the vast, and expanding, academic literature on negotiating. This is a deliberate choice and does not reflect either ignorance of the literature or lack of appreciation of its contribution to understanding. It is simply a case of 'horses for courses'.

Our wives, as ever, deserve most credit for the longest run of support and we jointly and separately thank Patricia, Anne and Kareen.

Glasgow
January 1980

GAVIN KENNEDY
JOHN BENSON
JOHN McMILLAN

1   Introduction

1.1   The prevalence of negotiating

We live in an age of negotiating. Almost all aspects of our lives are subject to some form of negotiation. Everybody negotiates, sometimes several times a day. We are so used to negotiating that we do not realise what we are doing.

Nations, governments, employers, unions, husbands, wives, lovers, parents and children all negotiate. Pick up any daily newspaper and mark all items that have anything to do with negotiating. You might be surprised at their number.

International politics, of course, dominate the news, whether it is a summit meeting between the Soviets and the United States or the Middle East negotiations between Israel and the Arabs, or any of a dozen important negotiations on sensitive issues (the Falklands, Gibraltar, French nuclear tests in the Pacific, the status of Afghanistan, or Lebanon to mention a few) around the world.

Unions negotiating new wage contracts with companies also attract extensive news coverage. Go-slows, strikes, bans and lock-outs are familiar dramas. Labour disputes are far more public than commercial disputes which occur with similar frequency but less visibility. Industrial relations disputes receive more publicity because both management and unions seek to win public support for their point of view. Commercial negotiations are conducted in private, partly to give competitors as little information as possible and partly to protect the companies' public images.

Over the past ten years there has been a substantial increase in the use of the term 'negotiating' in a commercial context. Negotiating in this context is not merely selling. It is an extention of the selling process once the parties have established their interest in doing business but need to agree the terms. It is not 'bid and offer' trading, common in certain commodity and service markets, such as ship chartering. Once commitment to the deal has been agreed, negotiating may well be used to complete the 'small print'.

Myriads of interest groups negotiate every day. Retailers negotiate their margins with their suppliers; they club together to get some bargaining leverage in buying co-operatives and they lobby the government to get relief from taxation or irksome laws, which were probably inspired by other interest groups in the first place.

Community action groups negotiate with their local government departments on property taxes, road crossings, traffic lights, welfare facilities, town planning, change-of-use zoning and, in public sector housing, questions of rents, tenancy rights and amenities. Local governments in turn negotiate with central government departments, largely about funding their budgets.

Most commercial dealing is underwritten by laws of contract. However, negotiating a contract is not the end of the matter — if it was, many lawyers would have much less to do. Circumstances can, and do, arise where the terms of the contract are open to differing interpretation or where something happens which is not explicitly covered by the negotiated agreement. Sometimes circumstances change in an unforeseen way and the contract requires renegotiation.

Injured parties, or their dependents, find it necessary to negotiate compensation claims, or settle the matter in court. Newspapers report only a tiny fraction of these settlements.

The judicial process is forced by congestion to resort to plea bargaining. This is more common in the United States than it is in the United Kingdom. A person charged with a serious offence will, through legal intermediaries, agree to plead guilty to a lesser offence in exchange for a smaller sentence. The advantage to the law enforcement authorities

2

COST OF UNILATERAL ACTION

Granada TV rentals objected when the Ford Motor Company introduced a new model and named it the Granada. Ford refused to withdraw the name. Following an unsuccessful court case, Granada Rentals retaliated by banning all Ford products from the company, which is a major fleet car purchaser.

is the certainty of a conviction against the uncertainties of a jury trial on the more serious offence.

It was common practice, not so long ago, for marriage settlements to be negotiated between the parents of prospective couples. The size of the dowry could be decisive, far more than the compatibility of the prospective partners. In poor countries the parents can secure themselves for their old age with well negotiated dowry settlements on their children. It survives elsewhere in form, if not content, in the attitudes parents might have to what they consider is meant by a 'sensible' marriage, or what we might mean by the statement: 'He (or she) married into money'.

Today, it is more common for negotiations to take place in a divorce settlement. Lawyers specialize in representing clients in these negotiations and they have recently extended their operations to cover negotiations when non-married couples separate. This in turn has created an interest in pre-marital negotiations on the criteria by which property will be divided in the event of a divorce or separation. The more interesting cases will be reported in the news along with other family-type negotiations such as inheritance claims. But, of course, the bulk of negotiating that occurs within the family is not reported. Domestic negotiations of this type are the most common negotiations of all.

The sexes spend a large part of their relationships negotiating. Husbands, wives and lovers negotiate or go under. Marriage involves a series of negotiated compromises because neither party has absolute power over the other. Parents deal with the world's most natural negotiators — their children.

A baby soon learns to negotiate the rate of exchange of noise for food. Later on, the child negotiates the relative proportions of cabbage and ice cream, where and when to play, what to watch on TV, when to keep quiet, when to go to bed and — quite separately — when to go to sleep.

Children usually are better at negotiating than adults because they have few inhibitions, they are prepared to use the sanctions available to them and they are only concerned with the present not the future. As adults we lose some of these advantages as our perceptions alter and we come to rely on our ability to articulate our views and thus attempt to persuade others to accept our wishes.

All these types of negotiations have the one thing in common which makes negotiating necessary: the parties involved have varying degrees of power but not absolute power over each other.

We are forced to negotiate because we are not fully in control of events. In circumstances where one person has total control over another it may be possible to dispense with negotiations (though experience of concentration camp regimes suggests that negotiating has a role to play even in those unhappy circumstances). Negotiating skills do not give you power where you have none nor do they allow you to ignore the trend of market forces. They do allow you to use what power you have more effectively.

What others do affects what we do. What others want affects what we can have. What we see, others see differently. What we think is in our interests, others think is against theirs. What we believe others should do is rejected. What we regard as necessary, others regard as inconvenient. Though we trust our motives, others do not. And so it goes on. Other people view the world differently from the way we do.

The right to differ is regarded in democracies as a fundamental right. Children, of course, exercise this right from an early age. They may not always get what they want but they seldom desist from demanding that their views be noted by their parents and each other. We carry this behaviour into life beyond the family circle. It pervades almost everything we do at work and at play. Given that everybody demands

4

the right to have a viewpoint, it follows that we must find a way of handling the mutual right to differ.

That is what negotiations are for.

Aside from conflicts caused by differing perceptions there are other causes of conflicts. For example, one of the parties might want to improve on the other's offer (even after a deal has been agreed) and introduces conflict deliberately. Sometimes there is a genuine gap between the parties outside their immediate control (fog delays the aircraft's departure; a major contract is lost; and in consequence, as there is no work available in the company, redundancies are inevitable). Conflict can arise because one of the parties say 'no' (for whatever reason), or they may wish to pursue a grievance they feel that they have because of an alleged failure in performance by the other party.

These situations, too, may be suitable for negotiation.

1.2 Alternatives

There are alternatives to negotiating. These alternatives are appropriate and even preferable in certain circumstances.

Decisions can be dictated by one party to another. If that party accepts the right, or might, of the dictators unilaterally to decide things then negotiating has no place in their relationship. Whether they accept this situation because they have surrendered their own rights voluntarily or because they are fearful of the consequences of non-compliance makes no difference. In these circumstances one party has been given, or has taken, unilateral rights over another.

Whenever this circumstance exists, decisions will be made without negotiation. Decisions by 'dictatorship' are far more common than is realised. The dictatorship does not have to be a personal one like Stalin's. The principle involved is the acceptance of unilateral decision-making and this is wide-spread throughout society.

In military service, orders are not subject to negotiation; in sport the referee's decision is final (though this does not prevent excited players challenging it, and risking punish-ment); criminals can force people to hand over their possessions on threat of harm; and we all tend to comply with the instructions of petty officials.

Employees may agree to accept instructions from managers for a consideration, namely their wages. On the basis of this contract the managers will make decisions unilaterally in specific areas of discretion (laid down in the contract or established by custom or practice) and the employees will carry them out. The managers will not expect to have to negotiate every decision they make with the employees for the duration of the contract. Negotiations are appropriate to change the contract but not to implement it.

When one has the power to take unilateral action it is sometimes tempting to do so. But where the other party is likely to be unhappy about accepting our decision, and resents it, they may be so reluctant to carry it out, that they attempt to get even when the power balance swings their way.

Joint problem-solving is another means of making the decision. This does not necessarily exclude negotiating, though negotiations may be required to agree to use this method on a particular issue and to decide on the agenda. Problem-solving requires a recognized commonality of interests between the parties and is not appropriate where the parties have and maintain different and conflicting views of the problem and the remedies. Some managers prefer to move a negotiation into a joint problem-solving session and nothing

---

PROBLEM SOLVING — WHOSE PROBLEM?

A teenager bought some new fashion shoes, but when he wore them for the first time his friends did not like them and mocked him. He returned the shoes to the store complaining that they were uncomfortable and asked for a refund. The store offered to replace them with an identical pair, which to their mind addressed the problem. This did not solve the teenager's problem but he could not admit to the real reason why he wanted to return the shoes as the store would have refused to accommodate him.

PROBLEM-SOLVING APPROACHES CAN CAUSE YOU PROBLEMS

A multinational corporation manufactured small domestic appliances in four European countries. All plants were of comparable size. Due to over capacity it had been decided to reduce the manufacturing capability by 25 per cent. The four national plant managers were called to a meeting to agree on this reduction.

The English management with their traditional sense of fair play came to the meeting with a problem-solving approach and failed to recognize the need to negotiate in this particular situation. 'We feel that each plant should bear an equal share of the cuts. We have examined our operation and have identified areas which we could eliminate.' The response was predictable. 'We are interested to hear that your operation can be cut. We have looked at our plants and feel that each is a wholly integrated unit and not amenable to partial pruning.'

The English factory was closed completely.

in this book will criticize them for doing so. Any criticism we might have is confined to those who confuse each method as if they were exactly the same.

Where negotiating fails to produce a decision it is sometimes possible to arrive at one through arbitration. A third party is designated to make a decision for the two parties who cannot agree on one. This may work but not always. Arbitration in some countries is legally binding; where it is not binding, an aggrieved party might renege on the decision and the dispute is back to square one.

It is also unpopular with negotiators because it requires that they give up their power to influence the settlement in their favour when they hand over the decision to a third and neutral party. Where the arbitrator's decision is mutually binding it has the characteristics of decision by dictatorship. Many contracts and agreements allow for the arbitration of disputes and this can act as a spur to finding an alternative to arbitration.

Pendulum arbitration is increasingly common. Under this regime, the arbitrator is obliged to select one or other of the final positions of the parties and is precluded from forming a compromise between them. This encourages both sides to move their 'final' positions close to what they think the arbitrator would regard as a 'reasonable' solution. They try to avoid appearing extremist in their demands, and therefore meriting a 'punitive' choice by the arbitrator of the other side's 'more realistic' position. Of course, in moving their final positions towards each other in case pendulum arbitration is invoked, they increase the chances of a settlement without the necessity of arbitration.

The most common alternative to negotiation is persuasion. It is often the first thing we try. If the other party can be persuaded to accept one's point of view, then the matter is resolved at no high cost and for little effort. Unfortunately, experience shows that persuasion has a high failure rate. People in conflict are seldom easily persuaded. Worse, the failure to persuade somebody often provokes feelings of frustration and anger ('Why can't the idiots see what I'm getting at. They are being deliberately difficult. Well, two can play that game!'). This can worsen the relationship between the parties rather than improve it.

We become convinced that our point of view is the right one and that the failure of the other party to agree with it is caused by a lack of understanding of it, or by an inability to use the same facts to arrive at our conclusions. As a result we waste hours of impassioned argument going over and over the same ground instead of negotiating to achieve a workable compromise.

Of course, persuasion occurs throughout negotiation. It is part of the process of communicating with the other party. But unless it is allied to meeting their interests it is unlikely to succeed on its own.

Conflict is uncomfortable, and we are often tempted to postpone dealing with it. Maybe it will go away, maybe they

8

will see reason tomorrow, maybe we will grow stronger if we let them sweat a while? Sometimes postponement does resolve the issue. They do go away, they do pay up, they do go on strike and save your wage bill, and your posting does come through before the auditors arrive. But as often as not, postponement merely puts off the reckoning. Things get worse instead of better. Negotiating skills are a glove that helps you to grasp the nettle of the problem.

1.3 Conditions for negotiation

Where two parties are in conflict there are a number of things they can do about it. They can, of course, decide to ignore the issue and agree to disagree. Differences of opinion on politics, religion and sport probably come under this possibility! But where these differences affect, or are part of, a work or commercial relationship, agreeing to disagree will not make the problem go away. If we want to do business we must come to some agreement on the terms of the contract — the conflict has to be resolved.

People negotiate because of self interest, be it corporate or personal. People move from their opening position because the other party has a sanction to force them to move or an incentive to encourage them to move. It may mean that a failure to agree involves high costs for one or both parties,

---

DIFFERENT FACTS

There is more than one set of facts. There are your 'facts', and his 'facts'.

If he repeats his version of the 'facts' he calls them 'hard facts'. Later they become 'well–known facts'.

Your 'facts' are described as 'guesswork', and on repetition, they become 'just your opinion'.

Further repetition reduces your 'facts' to 'irrelevances'.

---

loss of a valuable contract, an idle plant in a labour dispute, or a divorce in a domestic crisis.

It is the balance of sanctions and incentives, and peoples' willingness to bring them into play that creates the power equation in the negotiation. Well prepared negotiators take account of these factors when planning their strategy and tactics. The poor negotiator who overestimates his power, enters into conflict, finds he has misjudged the power balance, and cannot find a way to back down without a severe loss of face.

Agreeing is not costless. Doing business on unfavourable terms is bad for profits, and if persisted in can lead to bankruptcy. Negotiators who are highly motivated to settle at any price, will do a lot worse than they need have. But there are other costs. The concession itself has an immediate cost, to which must be added the longer term costs of the precedent set by the concession and the way it was made.

If a negotiator concedes a higher than normal discount he has also set a precedent and when the contract is next negotiated the customer will regard the discounted special price as the base for the next negotiation. If other customers hear of the special price they will insist that they benefit in the same way. If a company concedes a union's demand to buy peace in the face of a strike threat it may find itself faced with the same threat at future negotiations, coupled with a strong belief on the union side that their threat will achieve results.

PRECEDENTS CAN COST — 1

A chemical manufacturing company decided to sell its surplus capacity output at a marginal profit to attract new types of customers and maintain maximum throughput. Its traditional markets in heavy engineering and shipbuilding went into rapid decline, leaving it in a position of total reliance on the low-profit business. This market continued to grow and each new customer demanded a price as low as his competitor.

PRECEDENTS CAN COST — 2

A customer returned some goods to his supplier. To avoid paying out cash the supplier agreed that instead of issuing a credit note he would give a 10 per cent discount on future orders until the amount was made up. At the end of this period the 10 per cent discount was removed. The customer objected, demanding that he continue to get a discount on all future work otherwise he would change suppliers.

PRECEDENTS CAN COST — 3

A Scottish newspaper group decided to have the stonework of their main building cleaned. This necessitated the erection of scaffolding while the cleaning was in progress. Newspapers were despatched from the side of the building and normally the lorries and vans would back into the despatch bays and the papers would be loaded by the employees who lifted the packaged papers from a gravity feed system and dropped them onto the lorries where they were stacked neatly by the drivers.

When that side of the building was being cleaned the scaffolding prevented the lorries backing into the bays and the papers had to be carried a few feet from the feeds to the lorries in the street. The despatch employees demanded a special payment for the 'inconvenience' of the temporary arrangements and they demanded it for everybody in the despatch function whether they were directly affected or not. They refused to work until they got the payment. The management agreed to pay everybody £5 a shift as 'inconvenience' money to avoid a strike.

Some weeks later the cleaning was completed and the scaffolding removed. The management withdrew the 'inconvenience' payments because normal working was now possible. The men threatened to strike unless the temporary shift payment was consolidated into their weekly rates. Faced with this ultimatum the management agreed.

The costs of disagreeing can be high enough to make negotiation as an alternative a more attractive solution to 'slogging it out' in a damaging strike or to terminating a commercial relationship with bad feeling and perhaps a damaged public image in a messy court case. The failure to agree may provoke the parties to raise the ante by stepping up industrial action, cutting off supplies or taking other measures within their control.

In negotiation the object will be to minimize the costs of settling consistent with the general policies of the company or interests of the party.

Negotiation is appropriate where there is a balance of advantage between these costs. This necessarily must be a subjective judgement. The balance of power between the parties will tend to relate to the extent to which each feels the cost of disagreeing outweighs the cost of agreeing. These costs may not be known for certain beforehand and negotiating is a useful means of giving more precise content to the estimates of these costs. In negotiation earlier estimates will be revised or confirmed which will identify relative strengths or weaknesses for both parties.

Negotiations will be possible as long as both parties consider that the benefits of resolving the conflict through negotiating are greater than the likely benefits of resolving the conflict through some other means. This obviously includes the decision not to negotiate at all or, if negotiations

---

PRECEDENTS CAN COST — 4

In the 1980s there was a series of kidnappings of business executives in the Irish Republic. The kidnappers intended to raise funds by means of ransom demands. The Irish government refused to bargain with the kidnappers under any circumstances and managed to persuade most of the companies of the kidnapped executives to adopt the same stance. The danger is that if they set a precedent by paying just one ransom, then a spate of kidnappings would be likely to follow.

PRECEDENTS CAN COST — 5

In 1982, the Soviet Union walked out of the arms control talks. They accused the United States of 'endangering world peace' because it had commenced to deploy cruise and Pershing missiles in Europe. This deployment was in response to Soviet deployment of SS-20 missiles. In 1985, the Soviet Union returned to the talks, having previously declared it would not do so until the US missiles were withdrawn. In 1986, the Soviet Union left the Iceland summit, declaring that there could be no progress in arms control unless the United States abandoned its strategic Defence research. It is unlikely that the Soviet Union will recommence talks in due course.

GREAT FAILED ARGUMENTS

'But I need it more than you do . . .'

'But that's not fair . . .'

'That wouldn't stand up in court . . .'

'If you would only listen to the facts . . .'

are under way, not to continue them if the likely terms of business are absolutely unacceptable, it not being inevitable that once negotiations commence the parties will come to a settlement.

There is unlikely to be a successful conclusion to a negotiation, or a decision to negotiate, where one party will not move from a stated position. A blanket 'No' to all proposals by one party makes negotiations impossible. This might be a case of obstinacy or a badly played tactic but where the other party believes it to be the final position of its opponent it will conclude that the gains from negotiating on that issue are effectively zero.

It may not be the fault of the party saying 'No' that negotiations do not take place. The fault may lie with the party wishing to negotiate in circumstances where the other party normally does not negotiate. For example, walking into Woolworths and offering the sales person a smaller price for a shirt than the one marked is unlikely to produce a negotiation. Woolworths does not normally re-negotiate its prices with each customer — the costs of doing so would far outweigh the commercial benefits. Woolworths fixes a price per item on a take-it-or-leave-it basis. If you don't buy, somebody else will. On the other hand an offer to purchase a thousand shirts at a discount price might be entertained by Woolworths, though it is unlikely that the sales person at the store counter would handle the consequent negotiations!

Negotiations are only possible when the parties in conflict are willing to move from their stated positions and when that willingness is made evident at some point, or points, during their contact. If neither party makes that willingness visible there is unlikely to be a successful outcome. How that willingness can be safely expressed is discussed later.

1.4 What is a negotiation?

Negotiation is a process for resolving conflict between two or more parties whereby both or all modify their demands to achieve a mutually acceptable compromise.

Another definition from the world of labour relations is: negotiation is a process of adjusting both parties' views of their ideal outcome to an attainable outcome.

It is not always possible to resolve conflicts by negotiation. In these cases other means might be used. Parties also have the alternative of agreeing to disagree. A potential employee may prefer not to accept a job at the offered wage or a potential customer may decide not to buy at the price asked.

Conflicts can be of two kinds in the negotiating context. There can be a conflict of interest. This occurs where the

14

> ## IS NEGOTIATION NECESSARY?
>
> It is frequently argued by ill-informed pundits that negotiations are an unnecessary ritual when all that needs to be done is either to 'split the difference' or 'state the maximum you can afford from the beginning'.
>
> Some years ago the Ford Motor Company (England) adopted a pre-emptive offer negotiation tactic. They announced that their offer was absolutely final at the beginning of the negotiations. The unions refused to believe that the offer was final and many of Ford's plants went on strike. Eventually, the final offer was accepted. The deal undoubtedly would have been accepted without strike action if Ford had negotiated towards it. They did not repeat the tactic.
>
> The fundamental lesson remains. To achieve agreements you must be prepared to negotiate. To negotiate successfully, you should not start as low as possible and hope, somehow, to finish with the 'best' agreement. Negotiators do not 'split the difference' (if they did they would open as far apart as they could get). Different agreements will result from different ways of managing the negotiations.

terms of doing business have not been settled or, having been settled before, are now being re-negotiated.

Labour negotiations on wages, numbers, hours and working conditions are examples of conflicts of interest. In the strict arithmetical sense a gain to labour is a loss to capital: the resources spent on the employees' remuneration package cannot be spent by the company on investment, executive remuneration or shareholders' earnings.

Commercial negotiations on price, quantity, quality and delivery are examples of conflicts of interest. The seller prefers a high price to a low one and the buyer a low one to a high one. Revenue from sales for one company is a cost for another.

The more one company pays for its inputs the higher the price it must charge for its products or the lower the profit it must accept. Again, arithmetically, what one side gains the other loses.

The other kind of negotiating conflict is the conflict of rights. This occurs where there is an existing agreement between the two parties but where a difference of interpretation arises.

In labour negotiations a dispute can arise over the application of an existing agreement. For example, did a telephone consultation between a production supervisor and a maintenance engineer at a week-end constitute a 'call-out' and if so, how much pay is the engineer entitled to under the existing agreement? The conflict is about the rights of the parties under existing arrangements, not about their interests in securing new arrangements, though this might follow if an anomaly is thrown up by the dispute which identifies weaknesses in the current arrangements to the disadvantage of one of the parties.

In commercial negotiations the conflict could centre on whether the terms of the existing contract have been met. Did one party fulfil its obligations under the contract, and if not, was it entirely its own fault or did the other party contribute to its failure? Again, this is a conflict about rights not interests. It may follow that a party will attempt to secure itself some specific cover in case a similar situation arises again by attempting to alter the terms under which it does business.

The essential aspect of seeing negotiations as a process for resolving conflicts is to centre on the issue upon which they are in conflict and not upon their relationship in total. Because parties differ on an issue it does not follow that they have no common interest overall, or no common interest in finding a negotiated settlement. This is sometimes misunderstood by people who recoil at the word 'conflict' — seeing it as synonymous with disruption, schism, feud, quarrel, altercation and violence, etc.

We use the word 'conflict' descriptively because that is what it is. Recognizing a conflict of right or interest is, in our view, a preliminary to resolving it. Denying the existence of conflict is a victory of ideology over experience. If a party's rights or interests are threatened they will seek to defend themselves in conflict with those who threaten them; if they seek to extend their rights or interests they will promote them in conflict with those who resist. This behaviour is normal and natural.

Negotiations permit these conflicts to be resolved without the overall relationship between the parties being jeopardized. In industrial relations there is a continuing relationship between the parties which includes, but is greater than, the specific issues that they are in conflict about at a particular moment. The continuing relationship acts as a constraint or boundary to their relationship; it forces both sides to come to some agreement eventually. Negotiation is about resolving conflicts within the overall and continuing relationship.

Similarly, in commercial relations between parties, their conflicts are resolved by negotiation in a way which supports their overall relationship. Conflicts on price, for example, are bounded by the limits beyond which one of the parties would prefer not to do business. The conflict is about the terms of doing business and once decided upon permits that business to be done.

The parties have a common interest in finding acceptable terms for their relationship but the main point is that this common interest does not mean that *any* terms are acceptable, and for as long as *any* term is unacceptable there is conflict between the parties until they agree terms that *are* acceptable.

In negotiating, each party has a veto on any outcome that is proposed by the other side; therefore to secure an agreement that is acceptable to both sides it is necessary for an acceptable agreement to include sufficient of each party's interests

---

HOLLOW VICTORY?

US air traffic controllers struck over their grievances with the Federal agency that employs them. President Reagan dismissed them and hired new employees. The new employees have exactly the same grievances as the old ones.

---

to avoid a disgruntled party saying 'No'. Negotiated agreements are voluntary agreements, for if they are not voluntary, one or both parties need not agree to them, for if you absolutely *must* agree to a proposition, it is not a negotiation.

2   The Eight-step Approach

Negotiations are about the movement of the opposing parties towards each other until they reach a mutually acceptable position. A trade union leader once described wage negotiations as 'both sides walking towards each other'. He added that he aimed to get the employer's side to walk faster and with bigger steps than his side.

2.1   The negotiating continuum

The idea of movement implies distance and this corresponds to the language of everyday negotiation: parties speak of themselves as being 'a long way apart on this issue' or conversely 'being close to each other', 'close to agreement', etc., and they often summarize what is happening in the negotiation by such claims as: 'we have moved a great deal' and 'you have hardly moved at all'.

We can use this idea of distance between the parties to illustrate aspects of the negotiating process in a way that will sharpen our understanding of what is involved and what we are effectively doing when we negotiate.

If negotiations imply movement it follows that we must have somewhere to move from and somewhere to move to. We move from our ideal position to a settlement point that is acceptable to both parties. Our opponent does exactly the same. It is the relative bargaining strength and skill of the negotiators that decides the position of this settlement point and how far we have to travel to get there. We may be compelled to move a lot while our opponent moves only a little, if at all, or *vice versa*. The skills of the negotiator are directed at moving the minimum distance commensurate with obtaining settlement.

We can illustrate this by a simple diagram (see Figure 1) which we call the Negotiating Continuum. If we assume there are two parties to the negotiation, A and B, and that each

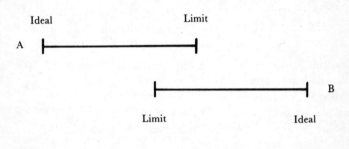

Figure 1

party given freedom of choice would select the position most favourable to his interests (his ideal) then these can be represented on the diagram at the extremities. Both parties, however, realize that they are unlikely to persuade the other to accept their ideal and thus will have to move some little way towards the other party's position. There is, however, a *limit* to this movement, sometimes referred to as the 'Break Point' — where the parties would prefer to break off the negotiation rather than to settle beyond their fallback or 'worst case' limit. This 'limit' may be the limit of the manager's negotiating authority. It may be the minimum price acceptable to do business or it may be the minimum quantity required to justify a production run. The range of settlement open to the negotiator lies between his ideal and his break point or limit. It can be seen from the diagram that the two lines overlap. Where these lines overlap then the possibility of a settlement exists. We call this area of overlap

20

the 'Bargaining Arena'. The settlement can be reached anywhere within this area, the final position being defined by the relative strength of the parties and by their negotiating skills.

This simple diagram is static. Negotiators often have cause to review their limit, as the negotiation proceeds, or to seek authority to move their limit. To go beyond this authority would lead to the repudiation of the negotiated settlement — in the case of labour unions, the replacement of their negotiators.

The prospect of disapproval, if not outright sanction or repudiation, acts as a constraint upon the negotiators when they contemplate settling beyond their negotiating limits. Circumstances might force them to go beyond their limits, but it is likely that the negotiators would seek authority to do so if they did not have total discretion.

'Seeking fresh instructions' is a legitimate reason for postponing a decision. Union negotiators often insist that their agreement is subject to endorsement by their members even when they are settling within their limits, it not being unknown for their members to reject a settlement on the grounds that the negotiators should have 'tried harder'. Commercial negotiators regularly insist that their agreement is subject to board approval.

The range between your ideal and your limit may be large or small. When negotiators talk about their 'room for manoeuvre' they are referring, in effect, to the range of possible settlements open to them.

It is important during the preparation phase to define the ideals of both parties and the limit of one's own negotiating authority.

In Figure 2 it can be seen that the lines do not overlap and that both sides could negotiate to their limits without reaching agreement. In these circumstances, the negotiation may become deadlocked. In this case one or both of the parties may use sanction behaviour to persuade the other to adjust his limit and thus achieve a meeting of the lines. This is most commonly seen in the form of a strike or a cutting off of supplies in credit.

The limits of each party are normally nearest to each other.

Figure 2

Figure 3

In Figure 2 the limits do not meet. There is a gap between each side which suggests that no settlement is possible for as long as this remains true. If the limit of one party is short of the limit of the other, either the parties will deadlock in their negotiations, or one (or both) will have to revise their limit, or get authority to do so, where the alternative of a breakdown in the negotiations, and all that might follow from that, is less attractive than settling beyond their initial limit.

It must, of course, be remembered that we are using this diagrammatic representation as an aid to understanding the complexities of the process and not as an exhaustive description of it. The diagrams prove nothing in themselves but they are useful as illustrations and they provide us with a simple language that corresponds approximately with the real world.

The diagrams are static and represent only a single issue. In the real world, negotiations are dynamic and involve many issues. This could be represented by a whole set of lines some of which overlap and some of which do not. An amicable

22

settlement may be reached if the parties agree on their principal objectives and abandon their lesser objectives.

In many kinds of negotiation it is not possible for the parties to know exactly what they want before the negotiation; sometimes their brief requires them to 'get what they can' and this may only become defined once the negotiations are under way; for example, negotiations with aircraft hijackers or kidnappers or any other opponent where the 'rules' and the 'stakes' are not clear before the parties meet.

It is also possible that the pre-negotiation ideal and the limit continuum has to be altered because new information emerges or new circumstances occur once the negotiations are under way. It has already been noted above that when negotiations show that there is no overlap between the limits of each party as in Figure 2, one or both parties will have to revise their limits if the negotiations are to be successful. Another possibility is shown in Figure 3. Here A's range overlaps B's ideal. If B discovers this during the course of the negotiations he will have a choice of settling at his ideal or revising it (revised ideal), as shown by the dotted line — if he does not 'discover this' he may settle for less than he needed to.

Negotiations differ from, for example, a game of cards. Negotiators are not bound to the hands they draw — they can alter their expectations during play as to what is an acceptable outcome for them. And they can revise in either direction — downwards because they discover that they are jeopardizing a settlement or upwards because their opponent is prepared to offer more than they expected him to before the negotiations began.

Once they are in the bargaining arena the outcome depends upon their bargaining skills — the more skilled they are the more their opponent will be drawn to settle near to his limit or, where their opponent's limit does not meet them within their settlement range, the more they will convince their opponent to revise his limit relative to their own.

The negotiating process is, firstly, about getting to the bargaining arena. Once in the bargaining arena it is about finding a settlement within it. Having discovered the possibility of a settlement, it is about securing that settlement at least cost and agreeing to its implementation.

The big question arises: what does the negotiating process consist of?

2.2 Understanding the negotiating process

We believe that negotiations can be seen as a loosely ordered sequence of distinct steps which can be presented to managers in a credible and simple form (the Eight-step Approach). Because these steps can be seen to be common to all negotiations and appropriate to all combinations of personality it is not necessary for people to first 'change the world' before they can use them. The eight steps provide a framework for coping with negotiating as a process and permit the development and practice of skills specifically related to each step.

Our approach to negotiating is not evangelical. We are not attempting conversion to a new way of negotiating. Our approach is based on what negotiators do, not what they ought to do. Nor does our method depend for success on negotiators only meeting other negotiators who use the same method. It is not like the truck drivers club of some years ago where a company offered drivers of its vehicles insurance for a token premium. They were covered for £1,000 in the event of their death arising from an accident while driving a company truck. This seemed a good deal until you read the small print; to qualify for the death benefit they had to be killed in collision with another truck made by the same company.

The Eight-step Approach is based on participation in, and the detailed study of, countless negotiations by the authors over several years and from the development of a successful negotiating skills training programme. Thus, the principles outlined in this book have been validated by the experience of negotiating in industrial relations and commercial dealings. In our view the only test of negotiation training is — Does it work in practice? We have proved that this approach works by monitoring the improved negotiating performance of many of the managers who have attended our courses.

The Eight-step Approach focuses on the skills of negotiating. These skills are set in real-world environments and successful training requires that the credibility of the approach remains high with practical managers (and cost-conscious training departments). Attempts to *train* management negotiators through abstract theories of negotiating and the use of extremely artificial issues (such as room changes or cups of tea) are, in our view, likely to be much less effective than the approach we have adopted.

In this respect our approach runs counter to the 'psychological school' of negotiator training, which is primarily concerned with the belief systems of the negotiators. It is popular with some managers because they believe that the source of industrial conflict can be found in the personality disorders of their opponents. This is crudely expressed in assertions that the other people are 'too stupid' to know what is good for them and what is good for them corresponds, of course, with what these particular managers find good for themselves. This is accompanied by statements of regret (if not nostalgia) about the way the world is drifting. Where this is joined to an academic approach which believes it has found the way to resolve industrial conflict by manipulating the behaviour of those involved it becomes a powerfully persuasive approach to prejudice.

The comments we could make about the various alternative approaches to our own would take another book as long as this one and breach our avowed purpose to avoid polemics or appraisals of the literature. We will simply assert that we do not accept the *training* value of alternative approaches, such as 'need theory' negotiating or over-complex manipulative bargaining.

Need theory implies that the negotiator is separate from the interests which he is presumably serving. Much the same is implied in transactional analysis approaches. Both may improve the interpersonal relationships of the parties, if only because divisive irritants are suppressed. But negotiating does not arise because the participants have somehow 'misunderstood' each other. It may very well be that their understanding of each other is precise and accurate and it is the understanding of each other that has created the need to negotiate their differences. In saying this we do not eschew 'good manners', we simply prefer not to over-rate them as the means to resolve conflict. We take conflict between the parties as a fact not as an obstacle.

Similarly, an over-complex manipulative approach leaves a great deal to be desired. The parties are expected to make estimates of the probabilities of various outcomes and then to calculate likely rewards associated with these outcomes, weighted by the probability of them occurring. This provides a spurious accuracy to the preparation of a negotiation position. In its most extreme form ('Game Theory') it is both illuminating and operationally limited. The negotiator is thrown back on subjective judgement — a guess. But the illusion of accuracy is maintained. The effort required to calculate the outcome is fairly demanding, especially under time pressure. It creates the possibility of a participant rationalizing practically any negotiating position or preference by manipulating either of the expected rewards to an outcome or the likely probability of its occurrence. If both parties are in error on these counts — both choosing mutually conflicting outcomes — we are back in the uncertain world of negotiation as represented by this book. In our view one might as well start there, without the arithmetical hassle.

We have by no means covered all the alternatives to our approach by what we have said so far. Nor are we so arrogant as to claim that our approach is exclusively the only one possible. All we are claiming is that it works and at little cost to a manager's sense of realism and his normal level of scepticism.

2.3   The Eight-step Approach

Our approach has been to take live issues that managers are familiar with in their daily work — wages, discipline, grievances, contract terms, price, quality, delivery, redundancies, budgets and so on — and 'speed up' the negotiating process by which they are normally resolved by concentrating on what the participants can do to advance their negotiations towards a successful conclusion.

26

Psychological 're-vamping' is not required. Nor is it necessary to invest in a study of behaviourism, or its off-shoots such as non-verbal body posturing, interesting as these subjects are. We do not concentrate on the 'furniture' of the negotiation, such as seating arrangements, eye levels, and other comforts. (Many negotiations take place in windy corridors and noisy workshops.) Training approaches based on these issues divert from the main purpose of training: to provide a framework through which the trainee (not the trainer) can understand what skills are needed and can practise them sufficiently to secure confidence to use them in the real world.

What then is the Eight-step Approach? Briefly, the negotiating sequence is broken down into the eight main steps through which negotiations will go, if agreement is to be reached, though not necessarily in a rigid order, nor with equal attention or time to each step. We make the central assumption that negotiations can be analysed within the eight-step framework whether the negotiators involved are aware of the eight steps or not. They will take minutes to learn, not days. They can be used straightaway and, more importantly, long after you are first made aware of them.

What differentiates one step from the next is the differing skills which are appropriate in each case. The eight steps are a map of the negotiating landscape. As with a map there is a relationship between the relative position of the features on it. But, as with any map, you do not have to start in the north, or the west, or the centre. The map's purpose is to help you identify your surroundings so that you may head off in the correct direction to reach your destination, which in the case of negotiating is to reach agreement.

There are four major topographical features in the Eight-step Approach. The four main phases are:

Prepare
Argue
Propose
Bargain

Within these four main phases there are certain minor steps. Within argument comes signalling, within proposing comes

27

packaging, and within bargaining come closing and agreeing. This gives the full eight steps.

1   PREPARE
2   ARGUE
3   Signal
4   PROPOSE
5   Package
6   BARGAIN
7   Close
8   Agree

We have identified four of the eight steps as the crucial phases of a negotiation, namely, PREPARE, ARGUE (or DISCUSS), PROPOSE and BARGAIN. If the negotiator fumbles these phases by inexperience, poor training, laziness or lack of practice, the resultant deal — if one is struck — is more likely to be a poorer deal than it need have been. For this reason we give special emphasis to the skills associated with these particular steps.

We will introduce and discuss each step in later chapters and the skill content of the techniques associated with each step will be highlighted along with more detailed comment on their role in the negotiating process.

It is our experience that people are able to absorb the necessary elements in each step with little effort and can use them to evaluate critically their current performance as a negotiator. They can also use them to evaluate what their opponents are attempting to do. Readers of this book will be able to grasp a framework for understanding their negotiations in one go and apply that framework immediately: they will know what is going on at any moment in a negotiation, where they want to go next and what they have to do to get there.

3 Preparing

3.1 Introduction

Preparation is the most consistent guide to negotiating performance. What you have done, or not done, before you arrive at the negotiating table will show up in what you do when you get there.

A badly prepared negotiator can only react to events — he cannot lead them. 'Let's see what they have to say' is the alibi of the unprepared.

A poorly prepared negotiator demonstrates sooner or later that he does not know what he is talking about. This will be recognized by his opponent whose confidence will increase and whose commitment to his own demands will be strengthened.

The art of management consists of knowing what has to be done and knowing how to get it done. The art of negotiating is the same and it is in the preparation phase that you define what needs to be achieved and decide how it will be achieved.

Too often preparation time is spent in rehearsing the arguments that the parties will use to defend their entrenched positions and attack the other party's position. The bad negotiator measures his success by the extent to which he scored points off the other (and is reassured by the intransigent attitude which this creates) in the belief that he is right and they are wrong. Constructive preparation is essential.

The salesman who prepares by calculating a range of discounts which he will offer, if pressed, may succeed in

29

obtaining the order but usually on the most unfavourable terms.

The personnel officer who prepares by estimating the least costly way he can keep the men at work will only teach them that he always responds to pressure.

All negotiators, whether in a buying or selling role or in a labour relations role, must look on preparation as a continuous activity and not as a one-day event prior to the negotiation itself.

The negotiator has to know his business, he has to know what he wants in the short term and in the long term. He has to know why he wants it. He also requires to be informed about his opponents' aspirations and circumstances. The industrial buyer must keep himself informed about his company, his suppliers, his suppliers' competitors and about his company's competitors. Management must keep themselves informed about the labour unions with which they deal, their politics, their personalities and their members, just as union officials must keep themselves informed about companies with whom they deal.

Company negotiators, incredibly, have been known to admit that they have seldom, if at all, read the union journals that circulate freely in their plants and often at the local library. How they can negotiate effectively with the union without knowing anything about it, must remain a mystery. For example, union militancy in one district may be more to do with a pending union election than anything connected with the feelings of employees in a particular plant.

It will be useful to consider preparation under a number of key headings which can serve as an agenda: objectives, information, concessions, strategy and tasks.

3.2   Objectives

The first priority in preparation is to establish your objectives. Everything follows from this. Parties may arrive at the bargaining table with all kinds of objectives but they seldom arrive there without having some idea as to the level of priority the objectives have. We accept that sometimes the

KNOWING YOUR OPPONENT

Trade Union Official

'When you've been negotiating with these buggers as long as I have, you get to know how they will react to anything you suggest, usually negatively. When they're nice they want something.'

Refinery Manager

'Hennesey never accepts anything first time round, and often not even second or third time. You can tell when he is about to say "yes" — his speeches are shorter.'

Civil Servant

'It took us several weeks to understand what the Chinese officials were up to when each of them kept asking the same questions. They were from different departments and each had to report separately on our answers. Hence, they asked the same questions.'

Contracts Manager

'With the XYZ Company, don't get carried away by their apparent keenness to agree with your solution to some problem they raise. There is always a "But" and the "But" means it is going to cost you something.'

principal objective will be to retain the *status quo* and also that the priorities may alter as the negotiations proceed. Preparation involves assigning relative priorities to your own objectives and questioning how realistic they are. There is little to be gained from aiming at the unattainable. You must also attempt to estimate the likely priorities in your opponent's objectives.

It is often difficult during the negotiations to establish what his priorities are. Indeed, he may make a considerable effort to conceal the fact that he has any priorities and will attempt to persuade you that everything he demands is of equal importance. The negotiator cannot complain at this form of bluff if he is also perpetrating the same bluff.

Remember your overall objective is to get as much of your package as possible by settling as close to your ideal as you can. But the very existence of a range of possible settlements between your ideal and your limit means that some of your objectives are less important than others and that you have a number of fallback positions.

This assumes that you have thought about this in preparation. Even if you have not thought about your own objectives — mistakenly believing that your demands are all equally vital to your interests — you will have to think about your opponent's objectives and how they are distributed among his priorities. The fact that his and your objectives differ has made the negotiation necessary in the first place and somebody will have to move if there is to be a successful conclusion to the negotiations.

If you assume that all your objectives are vital and he assumes the same, and each of you further assume that the other party will move, somehow at sometime, you are in for a deadlock (neither side apparently being prepared to move) or a long session (during which both of you will have to do the preparation you avoided in the first place).

Doing your preparation while you are negotiating is the worst option because it limits your ability to test the information that is being given to you by your opponent about his objectives and his intentions. Preparation should provide you with information about your opponent which you can validate during the negotiating sessions.

Opponents might tell you that unless they get such and such 'the union members will vote for a strike', or 'your competitors' proposals will look far more attractive' and so on. How do you know whether this is true – by the way your opponent says it, how heated or sincere he sounded, etc? That of course is one way. It is also thoroughly unreliable.

Another way would include research into opinions on the shop floor, or close study of the market for whatever it is you are selling or buying. This research is part of your preparation.

Of course, you must also be aware that your opponent can manipulate the flow of information to you by deliberately setting out to campaign for issues long before the formal negotiations. A union in the engineering industry regularly calls upon its branches to progress into the procedure systems all manner of issues and to pursue them through every level. This 'warm up' behaviour is aimed at influencing the employers before the negotiations. But again, only a properly prepared analysis of what is going on will give accurate information to the negotiators on what is an expression of genuine feeling and what is a ritual 'warm up'.

It is this aspect which makes preparation an all-year-round activity. Gathering intelligence about the other party ought to be elementary no matter what it is that you are negotiating about. You must not assume that your opponent arrives at the negotiating table straight from a sanitized environment, totally united in his interests and objectives. We can think of no groups containing more than three people where there is not some divergence of view. The larger the group the greater the likelihood that some members of the group will disagree with the leader's position.

Some members are bound to have different priorities and different measures of achievement. They are susceptible to different pressures, may have different aspirations and may have different estimates of what you will settle at. Lack of knowledge about these aspects of your opponent where much of that information is in the public domain, or at least readily available with a bit of effort on your part, is a handicap for which there is no excuse.

33

It can be seen that information plays a vital part in outlining your objectives.

3.3   L-I-M

Only you can decide what your objectives are in a negotiation. By setting out your objectives you are in effect also defining the criteria by which you will judge whether the negotiation has been a 'success' or a 'failure'. You are also self-selecting the likely level of resistance of your opponent to whatever it is that you are proposing, hence the temptation to select 'soft' objectives — aiming low instead of high — common among negotiators who lack confidence in themselves or their proposals or who are intimidated by their opponent before they even meet him.

Nelson said at the battle of Copenhagen in 1801 that the Danish defences 'only looked formidable to those who are children at war' and 'I think I can annihilate them: at all events, I hope to be allowed to try'. What a contrast between this Nelsonian spirit and those negotiators who give up valuable positions before they have tried to defend or use them to win concessions from their opponents!

Objectives must be realistic. They must have some credibility. Circumstances may be present, or unfold during the negotiation, which will prevent some or all of the most favourable objectives being reached. Experience and detailed planning of your case will assist your selection of realistic objectives. So will the L-I-M approach.

What do we mean by L-I-M?

Start out by making a list of your objectives — all of them, even those which are more implicit than explicit (keep your job, avoid a war, keep the existing business and so on). When the list is complete it could be defined as your ideal solution — what you would *like* to achieve. Many of the items on the list may be things that you already enjoy, the rest will be those still to be achieved. You must recognize that in any negotiation all the issues may be re-opened and it is possible to lose some items which previously have been taken for granted.

34

Recognizing that all of your objectives are unlikely to be attained, it follows that some will have to be abandoned as the negotiation progresses. Which ones? The answer must be the least important, the 'like to achieve' items. This does not imply that they have to be abandoned in total. They may only be reduced. For example: from 100 per cent of the contract and twelve weeks delivery to 100 per cent of the contract and ten weeks delivery.

Having identified the least important objective, you can then define those that in normal circumstances you would expect to achieve – those that you *intend* to achieve. For example: 75 per cent of the contract, list price less 12 per cent, and ten weeks delivery.

There is often a considerable amount of flexibility in this area. For example, 50 per cent of the contract at list price, 75 per cent at a 12 per cent discount, or 100 per cent of the contract at a 15 per cent discount.

All of these positions may be equally acceptable options. Alternatives such as these can be extremely valuable to a negotiation, and we shall return to them later in the chapter on bargaining.

It is now time to identify the *must* achieve objective. This is sometimes called the 'bottom line', or fall back position or limit position. These are objectives without which you would prefer not to reach agreement.

It is often very difficult to be precise about these objectives. For example, if 42 per cent of the contract is just acceptable at 18 per cent discount, is 41.5 per cent of the contract not acceptable? In other words, at what point do we walk away with agreement? Some tough negotiators spend their time probing their opponent's limit positions.

The objectives set in any negotiation are only fixed at a given moment in time. Circumstances, people, power, time, information and so on can alter the objectives, and their ranking and it is essential that they are kept under constant review.

Beyond the intend objectives you have your like objectives. These are the even more ambitious objectives you would hope to achieve in the most optimistic of circumstances but if they

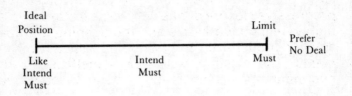

Figure 4

have to be sacrificed in the course of negotiations you are not going to get over-excited or self-critical about this.

Slotting objectives into the L-I-M frame will force you to consider the balance of forces between yourself and your opponent. This is of necessity a subjective exercise. You may overestimate your own strengths and weaknesses and under-estimate your opponent's. You may totally fail to identify correctly what the real balance of power is between you. Your opponent may 'irrationally' prefer a poorer deal than the one you are offering, or 'irrationally' choose to exercise an expensive sanction on you which does more damage to him than the eventual concession it might extract is worth.

Consideration of the relative strengths and weaknesses of the parties will assist you in assessing the relative priorities and realism of your objectives. You should abandon the most unrealistic before negotiation commences because putting forward utterly unrealistic (i.e. not credible) proposals often antagonizes the other party into equally unrealistic demands. This prolongs the negotiation and encourages deadlock.

In preparing your own L-I-M list you should also be thinking about your opponent's L-I-M list of objectives. If these are not immediately obvious they will become so in the early stages of the negotiation. They will also become more

36

CHOOSING OBJECTIVES

A major company decided to reorganize a very large production operation. The task involved the progressive closure of one very large factory with a highly militant workforce and the opening of three smaller, modernized and technologically advanced plants. The existing factory was inefficient with overmanning, demarcation and restrictive practices.

The ideal situation would be to achieve the closure of the existing operation and the opening of the new plants; to effect reductions in manning to economic levels and to introduce more modern technologies of work. Since negotiation implies an inability to achieve the ideal position the company's objectives could be classified thus:

L = The company would LIKE TO GET immediate reductions in the manning levels.
I = In order to remain competitive the company INTENDS TO GET the new technologies into operation at the new sites.
M = The company must produce and sell to survive. The MUST GET objective therefore is to achieve continuity of production. It is no good being 'right' in an empty factory.

The negotiating plan could involve trade-off between the objectives so that the short-term reductions in manning — an emotive inhibition to negotiating success — might be avoided by the union in exchange for the establishment of the new plants working smoothly with the new technology. A long-term agreement on natural wastage in manning over a period of time could be sufficient to guarantee overall success in the negotiation.

precise as the negotiations go on and you will have to assess continually, on the basis of what you see and hear, just how committed he is to his objectives. This requires your thought and attention in preparation, to some extent assisted by the necessity for you to make some judgements about your opponent's likely reactions to your own set of demands.

Negotiators often fail to define a true limit position given the circumstances. They set their 'limit' as a position they would like, not one they must get if they are to do business. Their 'limit' is often too high. It is as if they believe it a weakness to define the worst case they would accept if necessary. They either walk away from a deal they should accept or end up negotiating in an area they have not prepared properly for. They assume the other party's objections are exactly opposite to theirs, which need not be the case. By holding out for their ideal position on all issues, they forego opportunities to trade-off in some areas (even going to their limits) for advances in other areas. By holding out for their ideal position they provoke sanctions, and if they move under this pressure only they create precedents.

CONFUSING YOUR OBJECTIVES

A tyre manufacturing plant situated in a depressed industrial area of Scotland was operating four night shifts a week (Monday to Thursday). The management required that an extra shift be introduced on a Friday in order to keep the plant competitive within the multinational group. The union refused to agree to this (like to achieve: no Friday night shift).

After protracted negotiations the company threatened to close the plant if the union refused to co-operate. The union refused to move in spite of repeated management warnings of closure. The management eventually carried out their threat and the workforce were dismissed as redundant. Thus, the pursuit of a *like* to achieve objective meant the sacrifice of a *must* achieve objective, namely the keeping of their jobs.

OBJECTIVES AND CONCESSIONS

A hot air ballonist planned a flight between London and Paris. He defined his objectives thus:

> 'I would *like* to make it to Paris in one hop but I certainly *intend* to land in France. At all costs I *must* avoid landing in the Channel.'

GRAND BAZAAR

On a visit to the Grand Bazaar in Istanbul one of the authors decided to buy a gold bracelet for his wife. Having shopped around he went to the bazaar shortly before leaving for the airport. At a gold shop outside the bazaar he found the bracelet he wanted and bargained to a price of 42,000 Turkish Lira (about £90). The shop, however, would accept neither credit cards nor Eurocheques and he did not have sufficient cash to hand.

Inside the covered bazaar he found an identical bracelet in a shop which took credit cards. Bargaining reduced the price from TL70,000 to TL60,000 (about £135) but below that price the shopkeeper resolutely refused to go.

Dilemma: to pay a 50 per cent premium but keep his wife happy, or to refuse and keep his negotiator's self respect? (The other two authors have agreed to leave the actual result of the negotiation to the imagination of the readers and simply note that our colleague was guided by the alternative that represented his *must achieve* objective!)

LIM IT!

Some of the cases a negotiator is called upon to defend are, on the face of them, extremely difficult. Nevertheless, for many reasons, they may be required to defend the indefensible. In such cases the likelihood of sanctions is extremely high. Therefore there is enormous pressure to reach agreement in order to avoid disruptive sanctions but equal if not greater pressure to defend the wider principle.

The L-I-M analysis is vital here.

A classic example is where a workforce accused a foreman of some 'totally unacceptable behaviour'. He was accused on more than one occasion of swearing and abusive language towards female employees. These charges were rarely corroborated by management evidence. Nevertheless strong feeling existed among the women.

Then another incident occurred.

There was an immediate demand for the dismissal of the foreman. Naturally, the management had to refuse and did so. An unofficial strike began. An apparently insoluble negotiation had to be conducted. The management knew that to dismiss this foreman would put all of their foremen at risk and indeed would provoke action from the supervisors' union.

The company had four objectives:

1   To achieve an immediate return to work.
2   To protect the confidence of management and supervisors.
3   To preserve the disputes procedure against unofficial strike action.
4   To gain time to deal unobtrusively with the foreman.

On the face of it these are all MUST GETS.

(Continued oppposite)

The union's stated objective was to force the dismissal of the foreman. The company established priorities for its objectives as follows:

L = To achieve a return to work without any concessions.

I = To show that unofficial strike action did not pay and thereby avoid repetitions of breaches of procedures.

M = To achieve a return to work and avoid repercussions by foremen and managers.

The union in the negotiations accepted management's strongly stated position that the dismissal of the foreman would not be countenanced under any circumstances. They countered with a demand that he make a public apology and be given a final warning.

This was also unacceptable to the company but movement had occurred and negotiations were possible. They assessed the union's objectives as being:

L = Be paid for the stoppage of work.

I = Achieve future protection from the foreman.

M = To achieve a public apology.

The management had to propose a package which took these union objectives into account. They proposed:

'If there was an immediate return to work and a signed acceptance that future complaints would be dealt with through agreed procedures, then the company would ensure that a future proven occurrence would result in disciplinary action against the foreman. In recognition of the acceptance of future procedures for dealing with such problems, an *ex gratia* payment would be made to the employees concerned.'

This did not meet the estimated 'must get' objective of the union but it did meet enough of the interests of both sides to secure an agreement.

3.4 Information

We have seen that a considerable amount of information is required to establish the objectives. However, some of this information will not be available in advance and you must consciously seek during the early stage of the negotiations to obtain this information and to validate the assumptions made.

Once you begin making assumptions about your opponent's likely reactions to your demands or about his likely objectives, you are already setting out your negotiating tasks for the early part of the negotiation. Making assumptions is one thing — acting as if they are absolutely true is altogether something else.

Assumptions are best guesses, and sometimes not even that. We have to make assumptions all day and everyday and because most of them work out we tend to get a little careless about some of them where the incidence of accuracy leaves much to be desired.

When we catch a train we expect it to arrive at our destination. Mostly it does. When we leave our car at a garage for repairs we expect to collect it in due course, not to have the garage deny all knowledge of receiving the car. (Few of us, however, will assume the car will be ready when they promise it.) And so on. When we leave our house we expect it to be still there when we return and certainly not to have somebody else claiming to live in it. These expectations are based on our assumptions of the world around us. Most of the time we are right.

We assume order and regularity because we experience it. Our assumptions have been tested. But in negotiating, our assumptions cannot be tested beforehand; they can only be tested in the negotiations and therefore our early tasks ought to include testing the assumptions we have made about our opponent's intentions and commitment. If we act without testing our assumptions about our opponent's position we may inadvertently spend a lot of energy (and perhaps some of our precious concessions) in resisting something he is not demanding or demanding something he is not resisting.

Under the heading of 'information' a negotiator must consider what information he is going to reveal to the other side and the timing and manner of its revelation. Certain information may cause the other party to review his objectives considerably. They may be shown to be totally unrealistic in the light of this information. Experience has shown that negotiators have a tendency to conceal information rather than to communicate it. This concealment can lead to hours of irrelevant argument.

It is lack of information which creates the need for negotiation in the first place. If you have *all* the facts then you will simply open at your opponent's limit position and refuse to move.

We rarely have total information, however, and this is what makes negotiation unpredictable — and fun!

It follows that the more information that you can glean about the other party (the going rate, the history of the relationship, their style of negotiating, her personality, his motives, her culture and so on) the better the deal that you will be able to strike. You must still face the negotiator's dilemmas — where to open, when to move and how far, when to stop and settle — but information helps you to decide what to do and when to do it.

The person who has the best information in a negotiation also has a lot of power. It would be wrong to assume that this means that information should be withheld from the other party at all costs. On the contrary, it is the giving of selected information to the other party that structures their expectations in the correct direction.

Information falls into two categories: information about what you want and don't want, and information about how badly you want it. Obviously, it is usually in your interest to disclose what you want and what you don't want. It is seldom in your interest to disclose how badly you need or want something as the other party could use this information to extract a high price for meeting your needs. But if you are not reasonably open about your priorities the other party might address the wrong issues and ignore your real needs. Thus, in preparation, you must consider whether or not to give information, and how you intend to give it.

You must also define clearly your ideal position, the likely settlement position, the limit of your negotiating authority, the concessions that you are prepared to trade and the financial and legal consequence of these concessions. In different negotiating environments the information required will vary. For your own purpose compile a detailed checklist of the information you have needed on previous occasions and use this as a guide for the future.

THE WRONG INFO

A harassed executive, loaded with heavy cases, walked into a leading international class hotel in Milan during a trade fair. He said: 'I've searched the town for a room and I can't find one anywhere. Do you have one?' 'Yes, we have sir!' was the reply. 'Good' said the executive 'Now what sort of discount would you be willing to offer to me?' His chances of getting a discount, having disclosed his predicament and desperate needs, were remote.

THE RIGHT INFO

On visiting a friend's video shop to buy a video disc system, a Lebanese businessman set himself the target of achieving a discount of around 33 per cent.

When he requested this discount his friend informed him that he, the dealer, only made 12 per cent gross on the systems.

Immediately the businessman was forced to review his objectives as his expectation of the discount he could realistically achieve was structured downwards by the information he had received.

3.5 Strategy

Strictly speaking we should now discuss strategy. However, it will be more useful to consider this topic later, in Chapter 13, when we have analysed the various steps in the negotiating process. None the less in the preparation phase your strategy will need to be mapped out: what game plan are you going to follow in order to achieve your goals?

Planning your strategy is an important part of preparation.

It is appropriate to sound a note of caution at this stage. Avoid making over-elaborate strategic plans, e.g. 'at move 36 we offer them the green one with 10 per cent off'. The danger of this is that your opponent probably does not have a move 36 in his plan. Remember he has not read the script you have written for him. A strategy might be compared with a decision tree (see Figure 5). You wish to move the negotiation from A to B. Your strategy calls for certain key decisions, key agreements and assumptions to be made, following the *x*s from A to B. Your strategy must consider the variety of patterns that the negotiation may take and if you find that the negotiation is taking a direction towards Z that you had not previously considered then it will be necessary to adjourn to re-examine your strategy.

Strategy must not become too inflexible. It must be able to respond to developments within the negotiation. In short, if it isn't working, change it.

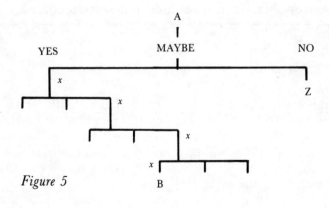

Figure 5

45

COLLECTING INFORMATION

A major multinational company is reported to utilize data processing to tabulate the incidence of issues raised by the workforce in the grievance procedure and the extent to which they are pushed to the various levels of appeal. This enables the company to make judgements about how important the issues in dispute at the annual negotiations are to the rank and file union member.

Armed with this pre-negotiation preparation the company is in a better position to make estimates of the seriousness of issues and how much the union will value concessions in these areas.

This enables the company to make judgements about what reciprocal concessions they can ask for or whether they should make any concessions at all. They can concentrate upon the vital issues for the other side and not be misled by what their opponents tell them.

On a smaller scale, any company can collect similar information by properly de-briefing its personnel officers on a regular basis, or sampling shop-floor opinion through the informal contacts between its supervision and the workforce.

3.6 Tasks

In the many minor day-to-day negotiations with which we are involved we act as an individual rather than as a member of a team. The more important the negotiation the more likely it is that each party will be represented by a group of people. It is, therefore, useful to consider the tasks that these people will assume in the negotiation.

Experience shows that it is extremely difficult to talk, listen, think, write, watch and plan simultaneously. (Some people appear to find difficulty in performing these functions singularly.) It is important to allocate certain tasks to members of the negotiating team. We call these tasks 'Leader', 'Summarizer' and 'Observer'. When you are operating in a team of two it will be necessary for the summarizer to take on the observer's tasks as well. When you are on your own you must undertake all three tasks.

The *leader* is the person running the face-to-face part of the negotiation. He, or she, may not necessarily be the most senior member of the team. There are, in fact, very positive benefits to be gained for the leader not being the most senior person. If the leader negotiates to the limit of his authority and is deadlocked then there may be a reserve position which can be authorized by the senior person. The danger is that the other party may realize that they are only speaking to the monkey and not to the organ grinder and that they may demand to speak directly with the senior person.

The leader's job is to conduct the negotiation. He does the bulk of the talking, makes the proposals, trades the concessions, and calls for adjournments. Leading is a demanding job and there are occasions where the leader wanders off the path, gets sidetracked, loses the thread of the argument, gets tired, loses sight of the objectives, gets bogged down in the argument, or is simply asked a question that he cannot or does not want to answer instantly.

This is where the summarizer comes into play.

The summarizer's tasks are to ask questions, to clarify, to summarize, to buy time, in effect, for the leader by keeping the negotiation on track. The summarizer can be invited to contribute ('What do you think, John?'), though the last thing you want from him will be an opinion! This is a coded request for assistance. 'Perhaps you could summarize the position, John?' is an equally valid invitation.

A well practised negotiating team will make extensive use of the summarizer. At no time will the summarizer attempt to take over the leadership. A summarizer can recognize when the leader is in difficulty and offer to come in. He can also draw attention to details that may have been missed by asking questions about them.

The third task is that of the observer. Undoubtedly the

hardest task to perform well, the observer's job is to watch, listen and record; to pick up the subtleties and nuances, and to 'read' the negotiation.

It has been evident to the authors over the years, in our negotiating skills courses, how much easier it is to be an 'observer' in the viewing room, watching the participants negotiating in the studio, than it is to observe as part of a team inside the negotiations themselves. Many things which are obvious on the video monitor are completely missed around the negotiating table.

We attribute this to the fact that the observers around the table are more personally involved in the issues and wish to make a contribution to the discussions. This means that a large part of their concentration is focused on what they might say if asked, rather than on effective observation of what the others are saying. The best method to concentrate the minds of observers is to ban them from speaking during the negotiation and require them only to contribute to the team during adjournments.

It can be appreciated that to combine the speaking part of the summarizer with the watching part of the observer is fraught with difficulty. When these tasks are combined with the task of leading a negotiation the difficulties are compounded.

MOUTH IN AUTO-PILOT, BRAIN IN NEUTRAL

Most salespeople operate solo and they evolve a technique of stalling for time while they gather their thoughts. They do this by trotting out a pre-rehearsed speech full of clichés, platitudes, waffle and technical bull designed to fill the silence with words while the brain decides what to do next.

A more effective technique is to summarize where the negotiations have got to and then *shut up* and think.

3.7 Checklist for preparing

- Use the following checklist in your preparation. Some items will need to be considered before the negotiation, some during the negotiation, some both before and during and they should all be reviewed during adjournments. They are not in any particular order.

Objectives	Priorities — LIMIT
	Are they realistic?
	Other party's objectives
Information	Issues, attitudes
	Power balance
	Personalities, precedents
	Interests, inhibitions
	Facts, assumptions
	To be disclosed?
	Does it structure expectations?
	In the right direction?
Concessions	Value
	Trade off?
Strategy	Keep it simple
	Keep it flexible
Tasks	Leader
	Summarizer
	Observer

- Set out your objectives in the negotiation.

Own interests

	Like	Intend	Must
1			
2			
3			
4			
5			
6			

Identify opponent's interests

	Like	**Intend**	**Must**
1			
2			
3			
4			
5			
6			

- What are the bridging factors that would make an agreement possible?
- What will you have to trade, or what have you to give, to promote an agreement?
- What fall-back positions do you have in case of difficulties?
- In what order do you intend to present your propositions?

3.8   Common avoidable mistakes

- Unprioritised objectives
- Incorrect assumptions
- Badly defined limit position
- Objectives too general
- Non-disclosure of useful information
- Strategy an end in itself
- Poorly defined team tasks

4 Arguing

4.1 Introduction

People negotiate because they have, or believe they have, a conflict of rights or interest with the other party. They are most aware of the conflict between themselves and the other party at the start of their negotiations, i.e. when the parties first meet to negotiate the issues in dispute. They are also most wary of their opponent at this time. It follows that the negotiations tend to be more tense in this phase.

Some negotiations do not get beyond the opening. They break down because the inter-party tension is heightened by the behaviour of the parties towards each other. Instead of coming closer together the parties move further apart, often resulting in the breakdown of the negotiation. The consequence of this is a strike, a lock-out or a lost order. These costs, which directly arise from the breakdown, may have been avoided if the negotiators had not indulged in negative behaviour. It is estimated that about 80 per cent of the time spent in a negotiation is spent arguing. Of course, a 100 per cent of the time is spent arguing in an unsuccessful negotiation.

4.2 Natural behaviour

People with different interests are likely to argue. This is natural. Most people are accomplished arguers and even saints can become emotional when interests close to their heart are threatened (witness Christ scourging the money changers from the Temple) which is one reason to be wary of those who forswear arguing — clearly they have short memories or nothing they value is threatened.

Some people claim that they do not argue but they will admit to discussing or debating. That is fair enough. It does not matter what name you use. We have chosen to call this stage *Argument*. In commercial negotiations it is more often called *Discussion*. Opening, presentation, exchange, confer are all alternative ways of describing this stage. However, we believe that the word *Argument* is the most appropriate as it indicates that both sides are involved. While the word often suggests emotional conflict it can also mean a rational presentation of the reasons for doing or not doing something.

Each party will give reasons why it believes something to be necessary, or seek to show by reasoning why something is true. They will discuss these conclusions and try to persuade each other by reasoning.

Of course, an argument can be a vexatious wrangle, row, quarrel or altercation. This is, in fact, the meaning commonly given to the word. If we said that Jones had an argument with Brown it is unlikely that you would have an image in your mind of Jones and Brown reasoning philosophically with each other. You are more likely to assume that they were violently disagreeing with each other. That is the beauty of the word argue. It can mean two distinct things, one reasonable and constructive, the other unreasonable and destructive.

And that is the point we want to get across about this step of the negotiating process. How you use the argument step will affect the progress of, and the outcome of, the negotiations. And arguing will not just be confined to the opening contact between the negotiators because the argument step can recur over and over again during the negotiation. Coping with argument, getting it to work for your negotiating objectives and not against them, will improve your performance as a negotiator.

The argument step is an opportunity not an obstacle. It can give you access to all kinds of information about your opponent's objectives, his commitment and his intentions,

LISTEN!

The importance of listening to the arguments of your opponent can be illustrated by the following example where a union raised an issue with a company engaged in warehousing in the packaged food industry. 'We are deeply concerned', claimed the union representatives, 'about the company's use of hired vehicles in peak periods and we demand that you stop using them. You are deliberately undermanning the depots and our members are being kicked from pillar to post trying to cope with the delivery problems that come up every week. You never take into account our feelings or the effect on our domestic life. The management never give adequate notice when overtime is required nor when it is cancelled. The scheduling is a complete shambles.'

Many negotiators would hear the demand from the union but not listen to their problem.

If they negotiated on the use of hired vehicles they might be trying to produce an agreement prejudicial to the interests of both parties. In the above example the real issue was the amount and allocation of overtime. Since no self-respecting trade unionist puts in claims to work overtime, he makes other demands. Realizing this enables the negotiator to see what amendments in the overtime rota will tackle the real problem.

from an invaluable source: himself. In argument you can explore the issues that separate you from your opponent, you can explore his attitudes, his interests and his inhibitions. An interest motivates an opponent to say 'yes'; an inhibition motivates him to say 'no'. His inhibitions and interests need not be obvious and you may be relying on your assumptions. This gives you a valuable opportunity to test the assumptions you made about him in preparation. If you know things about his position that he doesn't know you know you can also test his openness, or, in the extreme, his integrity.

Argument will reveal your opponent's inhibitions if you use the time effectively. It will also reveal your own. Argument is an exchange between the parties which can establish the benefits of negotiating a settlement or it can show that no settlement is either possible or desirable. It is remarkable how many negotiators forget about the former and act as if the latter is inevitable, though, when you ask why they behave that way, they insist in all seriousness that their behaviour was aimed at achieving the former!

4.3 Improving behaviour

One of the simplest and most positive steps you can take to improving your negotiating performance is to eliminate from your behaviour the habit of interrupting your opponent. People who interrupt someone are effectively telling them to 'shut up' ('Don't speak while I'm interrupting!'). Naturally, the person who gets this message resents it and before long a shouting match develops. For some parties in negotiation, shouting at each other is the norm, expletives included. Each treats the other with lack of respect.

If you ask managers why they behave towards their opposite number in this way they reply: 'It's the only language *they* understand'. Maybe it is the only language they have been taught?

The commercial equivalent of 'bash the other side' behaviour is the negotiator who ignores his opponent's interests, presses on with his own, interrupts whenever he thinks the fool he is dealing with has waffled on enough, cuts through objections, denies liability, acts arrogantly and generally behaves as if the other party is being done an immense favour by being allowed in the same room. (Those sellers who think we have just described the typical buyer will be surprised to know that many buyers believe we have just described the typical salesman!)

Destructive argument is all too frequent an experience in the opening step of the negotiation and sometimes as frequent

GOTCHA!

What does somebody do when they want to cross a busy road? Watch the traffic? No, they watch for gaps in the traffic so that they can cross safely.

Negotiators in discussion also watch for gaps. They watch for gaps in the other negotiator's flow of 'facts' so that they can make their own views known. Naturally, each statement they make ignores any other statement made by the other negotiator. Two monologues, not a dialogue, take place in the same room.

in the other step as well. It is common in industrial relations but also in commercial negotiations on contract reviews, liability disputes and inter-departmental wrangles over resources.

Where people are highly committed to something, or angry, disappointed or anxious, or insecure or just plain fed up with something, they are likely to charge at their opponents like wild elephants or, just as damaging, sit back and pick them off with studied, wounding blows.

Point scoring is a temptation few can resist. Sometimes you await your chance to get in with a destructive thrust: 'I am not going to let you get away with what you said ten minutes ago', or 'You accuse our side of incompetence, what about when you lost a consignment last June, you weren't so bloody clever then were you?' And so it goes on, each side sniping at the other.

The attack-defence cycle and the blame cycle are well established features of destructive argument. If you attack somebody they will inevitably defend themselves no matter how trivial or irrelevant the attack is compared to the main objectives of the negotiation. If you seek to apportion blame incessantly in the meeting your opponent will either emotionally resist the charges or attempt to pass the blame onto you like the pass-the-parcel game at children's parties.

Once an attack-defence cycle gets going the parties queue up to get their thrust in. The faster the attacks, and their replies (normally accompanied by interruptions), the higher the emotional tension. Personal accusations will intrude ('Are you calling me a liar?') and affect the interpersonal relationships, perhaps damaging them beyond repair.

People in an emotional state make threats, not necessarily intending to carry them out, but threats provoke counter-threats and the parties may end up in a mutual exchange of sanctions because they have boxed themselves into corners from which a retreat would cost them too much loss of face. Moreover, people resent being threatened and the making of threats is likely to worsen the relationship rather than improve it. Forcing someone to bend to you by the use of a threat is likely to leave them waiting to retaliate when the balance of power shifts.

A shop steward at a car plant expressed the resulting relationship between his members and the management in the following way: 'When you need cars we screw you, when you don't need cars you screw us'.

If negative argument behaviour is endemic in your negotiating environment it is more than likely the consequence of a long period of argumentative behaviour, with mutual shortsighted sanction exchanges on specific issues when neither side felt strong enough, each event reinforcing the stereotyped image the parties have of each other: 'As you sow, so shall you reap'.

Negative argument reinforces the inhibitions of your opponent. These inhibitions prevent an open negotiating stance and sometimes prevent an agreement on an issue even when agreement is mutually advantageous. If each side is solely concerned with 'winning' it must regard every concession to the other side as a 'loss', no matter how minor.

The consequence is that both parties get nowhere except further apart which is the antithesis of negotiating.

4.4 Constructive behaviour

As always the remedy is fairly simple: listen more than you talk. Now that is easier said than done. And by itself it is not enough. Positive listening behaviour has to be supported by positive talking behaviour: when you do talk make sure you use the time effectively. One way to do this is to ask open questions which encourage your opponent to explain and elaborate upon his case.

From your preparation you know your own point of view on the issues but what you do not know yet is your opponent's point of view. You have made estimations in your preparation and now in the argument step you have the opportunity to test those estimates. This is made easy by the fact that he is normally very keen to tell you his views. Encourage him to do so.

Your opponent may not be ready to tell you everything. Nor may he be prepared to divulge to you anything about his limit position. He will be trying to convince you that his opening position is his limit. That is why parties at the opening escape so easily into unproductive argument — it helps prevent their opening positions from being probed too deeply. Hence, the more you can get him to talk about his position, by aiming questions for clarification and explanation, the more he may inadvertently give clues away about his commitment to his position and the possible lines along which he is prepared to move.

In asking open questions you must avoid provocative language otherwise you may go down a snake instead of up a ladder. The question: 'How do you justify that outrageous joke of a demand you have just made?' is more likely to provoke an emotional defence (which tells you nothing) than tell you what you need to know about his reasoning and how sure he is about his demands. Far better to put the question into the form: 'Could you explain the basis upon which your claim has been drawn up?'

Having discussed the basis of the claim it is useful to go over the claim in detail, asking questions on every point and exploring the implications in your opponent's mind of each part of the claim, being careful not to plant ideas in his head he had no thought of up to then. This will bring out 'hidden costs' in the claim, or proposal, and make them explicit early on. A five-point claim with twenty implications, each of which involves costs, widens the scope for creative negotiating and

57

Customer: 'This artwork is totally unacceptable. There is no way I am accepting your corporate name and logo on my company's ID card.'

Option one
Supplier: 'Well I am very sorry, but our name and logo appear on all of our products and our price takes account of this.'
Customer: 'In that case I shall take my business elsewhere.'

Option two
Supplier: 'Can you explain to me the basis of your objection?'
Customer: 'For a start, your name runs at right angles to the card text, it's in a darker colour, and it is right in front.'
Supplier: 'So, if we turned our name round, printed it in reverse in a paler colour, you would be happier?'

forms the basis for a response which can use the mutually explored costs to build an alternative proposal.

Before responding to a detailed claim of this nature it is appropriate to summarize your opponent's position by asking him to do it or by going through it yourself, drawing attention to any agreed implications and his (not your own) attitude to them.

A summary is always useful, especially where the issues are numerous and complex. It cuts through confusion and negative argument too. 'Let us summarize what you are asking for' is positive behaviour. It helps to re-focus the negotiations if they are wandering. It gives your opponent the important feeling of being at least listened to with respect no matter how outrageous, or ambitious, his demands are. Remember he too places an order of priority on his demands. He too includes things he would like to get as well as things he must get. He dresses up his demands with things he will sacrifice to get what he wants but which he will gladly accept if you insist on giving them. He too will avow that his first offer is exactly what he wants to settle on — he is most unlikely to say: 'No, I don't really want what I have just asked for, I've got a limit position in my briefcase which if you ask me I would be delighted to tell you about'. But he does want to be taken seriously. He expects to negotiate and not be rejected out of hand with emotional attacks, sarcasm, threats and abuse.

4.5 Constructive response

Your response is the other side of what you have got your opponent to do for you. It is to give information to your opponent about your position. If you have extracted information from your opponent in the way suggested above you are in a better position to respond to his declared position and to explain your own.

Your response may be a detailed alternative to your opponent's claims or offer. It may be a detailed amendment to his proposed terms for doing business or amendments to a proposed contract. You may rank items in his proposals which you cannot agree to at all and those which you are not in agreement with at the moment but you are prepared to negotiate if they are amended. You may reply to each of his points and the implications of them and state why you cannot accept what he is suggesting.

The form of your response will obviously depend upon what kind of negotiation you are involved in. His claims may be subject to your counter-claims (a liability negotiation), his claim may be subject to an alternative offer (wages negotiation), his demand price may be subject to your buying price (a sales negotiation), his tender may be subject to your re-packaging (a contract negotiation), his position may be subject to your rejection of it in its present form (a change of status negotiation) and so on.

But all of these responses, in whatever form they take, are setting out the opposing ideal positions of the parties. No matter how long the argument step goes on for, with each side deploying arguments to support its position and oppose the other's, no progress can take place in the form of a movement away from these positions unless and until the parties indicate their willingness to negotiate something different from what they are both offering.

If you have not explained your ideal position then there is little likelihood that the other side will be prepared to move towards it. There is a reluctance to set out on a journey if one does not know the ultimate destination, and while in negotiation you will not travel all the way to the other side's ideal position it is necessary to know its location so that you can assess how close to your limit it is.

Management often face this problem in pay negotiations. They know their ideal position and their limit in advance. However, they may have no official information as to the union's ideal position. The claim may be for 'a substantial increase in wages'. This arises because the unions may not know how much the management are prepared to offer and may be afraid to ask for too little.

In explaining your own position you are not precluded from opposing your opponent's. That is not what you should refrain from doing. Our point is that if you merely oppose destructively you will delay the negotiations moving subsequent stages of the process by which mutual agreement will be eventually reached.

It is perfectly legitimate for you to explain why you oppose all or anything that your opponent presents for consideration in the negotiations. Indeed, you would be weakening your own negotiating position if you did not do this. By challenging your opponent's position *as it stands* you are not undermining the negotiations at all, in fact you are preparing the way for movement if you use the productive behaviour discussed above.

In challenging your opponent's position and explaining your own you are creating a platform from which the next steps in the negotiation can take place. You establish in opposition the strength of your commitment to your own position.

If you have identified your opponent's inhibitions, commit-

YOU GET WHAT YOU ASK FOR

An accountant and his brother were into breeding racing cabbages. The largest cabbage on a specified date was the winner. One season, his brother's cabbage grew up to be a cauliflower and he was disqualified. He wrote to the seed supplier complaining about his disqualification and stated that he thought his inconvenience was worth £20. A cheque arrived for £20.

Another accountant, overhearing the story, reported that a similar disqualification had been imposed on him, and when he wrote to the seed merchant and complained, he received a letter of apology and another packet of seeds.

Moral: specify what you want and you have a good chance of getting it.

THE OPEN DOOR

Effective negotiators avoid closing doors. A straight forward 'No' slams the door shut. On the other hand 'If we were to consider that, what would you be offering' keeps it open.

'Let us say that we agreed with that proposal, what would you . . .?' looks beyond the immediate issue without committing you.

'Is there any other information that you feel I should have at this time?'

'Why is that important to you?'

Asking open questions unlocks doors — listening to answers opens them.

ment and intentions you will have formed a judgement about the possibility of negotiation on the issue of dispute. If that possibility exists then you can proceed to negotiation. How you manage the next step from the argument will be discussed in the next chapter.

4.6   Checklist for arguing

- *Avoid:*
  Interrupting
  Point-scoring
  Attacking
  Blaming
  Being 'too clever'
  Talking too much
  Shouting your opponent down
  Sarcasm
  Threats

- *Practise:*
  Listening
  Questioning for clarification
  Summarizing issues neutrally
  Asking opponent to justify his case on an item-by-item basis (watch for signals)
  Being non-committal about his proposals and his explanations
  Testing his commitment to his positions (looking for clues about his priorities)
  Seeking and giving information (be careful about unintended signals)

4.7   Common avoidable mistakes

- Not asking open questions
- Not listening
- Arguing to 'win'
- Scoring points

- Interrupting
- Circular argument
- Not summarizing
- Not validating assumptions

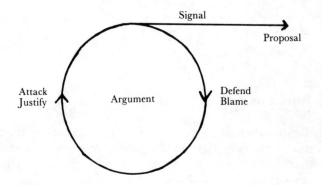

Figure 6

5   Signalling

5.1   Introduction

Negotiation is about movement. Parties must move towards
each other – or one party may agree to move on one issue if
the other party agrees to move on another issue. But move
they must if the negotiation is to be successful. The problem
for negotiators is how to achieve this movement: in essence
how can we ensure that any movement is matched by a
movement of the other side? The principal motive forces in a
negotiation are the sanction and the incentive — or to put it
another way, the penalty of not agreeing and the benefit
of agreeing. These forces may be implicit or explicit in the
negotiation. It may be necessary to draw attention to the
consequences of agreeing or disagreeing.

5.2   Conditions for negotiation

The motive force behind negotiation is self interest, be it
corporate, national or personal. We negotiate because the
other party has an incentive to offer us or a sanction to use
against us. Without either of these, people don't or can't
negotiate.

The parties may begin by stating their total commitment
to their position and total unwillingness to make concessions.
However, their presence at the negotiating table signals a
willingness to do a deal.

The first thing we have to do is to understand the nature of the problem and from this the nature of the remedy. Deadlock could be occurring because each party has adopted the strategy of sticking to their opening position until the *other* party indicates a willingness to move. If both parties stick rigidly to this strategy there can be no movement.

But why should one party, let alone both, adopt such a strategy? Surely, it pays to indicate willingness to negotiate, i.e. move from a stated position? Of course it does, but not all negotiations start from a recognition by the negotiators that it is *their* position which is negotiable. Moreover, there may be considerable distrust or tension between the parties because one party sees its interests as being served best by maintaining the *status quo* and resisting any change at all.

Some parties may insist upon everything being negotiable

THE INFORMAL GO-BETWEEN

A computer company was due to move a part of its administration to a new office block. Two department heads were in dispute over the amount of floor space each department should receive. The R&D Department reported to corporate HQ in the United States and the Sales Department reported to the European HQ. There was no single manager based locally with authority over both departments.

The dispute was bitter, each fielding strong arguments and giving no ground. The slightest signal was probed to the point where it was withdrawn.

An external management consultant who was working with both departments on an unrelated project became the confidant of both managers. Each sought to recruit him as an ally. The consultant was able to perceive the signals from each side and without favouring either he acted as an informal go-between until a formula for resolving the issue was worked out.

CONCILIATORS AND MEDIATORS

Signalling is a skill which sometimes has to be carried out by a third party. The role of the third party does not change the eight-step analysis of negotiation.

The conciliator or mediator simply takes over the signalling role of the parties in conflict. Thus, where one or both parties are unable, incapable or afraid to signal a change in their ideal position, they may seek (or be compelled under their rules of procedure to seek) the assistance of a conciliator to do their signalling for them.

This is common in both industrial relations and in international diplomacy. In the UK, the government's Advisory, Conciliation and Arbitration Service (ACAS), recognizes industry's need for independent signallers. In the Middle East, the United States has performed the role in numerous attempts to get peace between Israel and its neighbours. In the dispute between France and New Zealand over the sinking of the Rainbow Warrior, the Secretary General of the United Nations acted as a mediator to arrange a settlement: France paid compensation and New Zealand released the French secret service agents.

The conciliator explores the stated positions of each side to determine what concessions one side might be prepared to make in exchange for concessions from the other side. In private, he then makes the appropriate signals to the parties in dispute. He must give the parties confidence that there is an opportunity to negotiate further without their positions collapsing.

and others on only very limited matters being negotiable. A company may be prepared to negotiate on the managerial right to make the final selection. The Israeli government may be prepared to negotiate on autonomy for Palestinian arabs in certain of its occupied territories but it may not be prepared to negotiate on autonomy where this compromises, in its view, the security of Israel. Britain may be willing to negotiate on anything with Argentina except the sovereignty of the Falklands.

But even if the items before the negotiators are in the category of being negotiable it is still rational for one or both sides to take a 'hard line' in the argument step and to give the impression that it cannot compromise on its opening position.

Why? Because it may not feel able to handle the situation where it makes concessions. This is not an uncommon occurrence in negotiations. Concessions can be taken as a sign of weakness; the first step along the road to surrender. Once you start making concessions there may be no stopping them, hence the best way to avoid this is not to make any concessions but wait for the other side to make its concessions and then pounce upon them. If you say 'no deal' long enough the other side will eventually surrender, etc. Of course, if you do pursue that strategy of waiting for the other side to concede as a prelude to it collapsing you may — and more than likely will — end with 'no deal'.

WILLINGNESS TO NEGOTIATE

In the presentation of the annual shopping list of wage claims the union negotiator stated in support of one item: 'It is union policy that our members should claim a shorter working week with a reduction in hours from 40 hours to 35 hours'.

The statement 'It is policy' is a signal that the reduction in hours is a *like to get* objective which can be traded off in the ensuing negotiations (and was).

The real key to this particular negotiating behaviour is the inability of the other side to handle concessions. This may come from lack of experience — novice negotiators are either 'pushovers' or 'stonewalls', they either throw everything away quickly or give nothing away at all. This way they either get lousy deals or no deals, until they gain the necessary experience.

5.3 Signalling behaviour

The way to handle concessions with confidence is to develop skills in signalling behaviour. This will give you the means to test an opponent's apparent stonewall position and establish whether it is based on his reading of the relative power balance or upon his lack of confidence as a negotiator. It may also be due to lack of information. This is the situation which salesmen will recognize under the heading of 'objections'.

The salesman is taught that there are two principal types of objection, real and false, and he is taught to test which category they fall into by asking the question: 'If we were able to overcome that problem, would you be prepared to buy?' If the answer is yes, then that is a real objection. If the answer is no, and another objection is raised, then that is also handled in the same way. Real objections can be handled in one of two ways: either by being set aside to be dealt with later or by being answered immediately. In the negotiating context this usually implies giving information or trading a concession.

A signal is a means by which parties indicate their *willingness* to negotiate on something. It is also more than that: it

---

THINGS YOU OVERHEAR

'Telex them and quote $364 a ton. No, wait a minute. They might say "no". Add that if the price is not acceptable, we are prepared to come down a bit . . .' (No prizes for guessing what response they got to that!).

---

implies a willingness only if it is reciprocated by the other side.

The advantages of signalling behaviour should be apparent. It can be used to 'break out' of circular and non-conclusive argument. Reciprocated signals ensure 'safe-conduct' for the party making fresh proposals without the fear that its conciliatory action will be taken as a surrender. Parties can then propose without losing face and without sliding down a slippery slope to the other party's entrenched position.

Using signals has the additional advantage that no new behaviour has to be learned because most of us already practice signal behaviour in our daily lives. True, we might do this unconsciously. That does not matter at all because once we recognize what we are doing *naturally* it only takes a little practice to do it *intentionally*.

5.4 What is a signal?

The dictionary defines a signal as a message. Like all messages it has to be interpreted by the receiver. The message may not be received, if received it may not be understood and if understood it may not be acted upon. Signals are therefore fragile and like anything fragile they can have a short and unproductive life.

Statements in the argument step are of an *absolute* nature: 'We will never agree to what you are proposing', 'We do not give discounts', 'We will not accept that change', 'No way', 'Not a wax cat's chance in hell', and so on. The characteristic of an absolute statement is the absence of qualification. Opening positions tend to be unqualified. Disagreements between parties in conflict tend to be unqualified. That is why the argument step can so easily get bogged down when unqualified opposition is expressed to another party's point of view.

Parties express themselves colourfully, and therefore provocatively, when they are using absolute and unqualified language. A proposal is 'nonsense', 'rubbish', 'useless', 'half-baked', 'laughable', 'disgraceful', 'out of the question' and so on, and the people who proposed it come in for equally

THE HIDDEN LANGUAGE OF SIGNALS

'We would find it extremely difficult to meet that dead-line'	— Not impossible
'Our production line is not set up to cope with this requirement'	— But it can be changed
'I am not empowered to negotiate this price'	— See my boss
'It is not our normal practice to break bulk'	— So who's normal?
'Our company never nego-tiate on price'	— We do negotiate what you get for that price
'We can discuss that point'	— It's negotiable
'We are not prepared to discuss that at this stage'	— It's negotiable — tomorrow
'We never admit liability'	— We only make *ex gratia* payments
'We could not produce that quantity in that time'	— I'm prepared to negotiate on price, delivery, quality, quantity
'It is not our policy to give discounts and even if we did they would not be as large as 10 per cent'	— I'll give you 2 per cent
'Our price for that quantity is X'	— Different quan-tity, different price
'These are our standard contract terms'	— They're nego-tiable
'That is an extremely reason-able price'	— It is our ideal position

extreme absolute condemnation — questioning their parentage, their intelligence, their honesty, their patriotism, their humanity and so on.

But watch a negotiation in its argument step. Listen to the language used. Somewhere, tucked away, sometimes in long sentences, you will hear a qualification used. That is a signal.

Signals are qualifications placed on a statement of a position. Instead of 'We will never agree to what you are proposing' the words 'In its present form' might be added — such disarming innocence, yet so vitally important for the progress of the negotiations. The negotiator is telling the opponent to amend his proposition in some way and if he does he will create the possibility of agreement. But note that the signal is not a movement by the party sending the signal, it is a call for the other party to move. Where then is the gain in that? The gain lies in what the party receiving the signal does about the message it has received.

Faced with total intransigence from their opponents the negotiators are being told in the signal that total opposition is confined to the 'present form' of what is proposed. This implies that the proposition in another form, *as yet undisclosed*, would not receive *total* opposition but would, in other words, be negotiable.

An elementary mistake at this point would be to try to guess which way the proposition must be reformed before the opposers are prepared to modify their total opposition. That would be like saying: 'So you do not accept my first proposition, fair enough, why don't we go through all the alternatives I have in my briefcase, including the concessions I can give you, and when we find a proposition which you can agree to, stop me, and we can settle on it!' Unfortunately, that kind of response is all too common. An excuse often given for responding that way is the all too familiar one that it is better than a breakdown in the negotiations. However, as a reward for intransigence it cannot be beaten. Opponents will learn (and quickly) to say 'no' and sit back while you throw everything at them that you have to offer in return for nothing more than their eventual agreement to whatever package suits them.

That is not what the message should mean for you, nor is

it how you should react to the signal. Re-read the signal: 'in its *present* form'. They sent the signal and they are in the best position to tell you what they meant by it. Why not ask them for more details? But make sure you do so by signalling back your willingness to consider altering your opening position if their movement is encouraging enough. It is no good saying: 'We are glad to note that you have seen the light and are withdrawing your total opposition to our perfectly sensible proposals'. They are likely to withdraw back to the argument and withold further signals because you have punished them for making one.

A far more constructive negotiating response would be along the following lines: 'If you are prepared to give details on the kind of amendments which would enable you to consider accepting our proposals, we would certainly be prepared to consider responding positively to what you have to say.' By saying something like this you open up the way out of the argument step. They are not asked to surrender their position, nor are you committed to accepting what they propose. Instead of arguing from entrenched positions, the possibility of movement has been created.

The signal has led to movement. That is its role. It is a device by which movement can become possible.

5.5 How to signal

Signalling requires that the participants are listening as well as talking. In fact most people miss signals — and therefore prolong the argument — because they *talk* more than they *listen*. If you do not listen to what your opponent says, and *how* he says it, you will inevitably miss his signals. If you are carried away with point-scoring and attack/defence and blame cycles, you will miss even the most blatant signals, driving yourself into a corner from which nothing will coax you. You may believe it is all your opponent's fault and so it might be but you too have a responsibility for signalling.

Consciously missing a signal involves a wholly different skill (and circumstance) to missing one through negligence. We call this 'blind-eyeing' the signal. Nelson 'blind-eyed' the signal from his commander to leave off action, i.e. withdraw, in the midst of a particularly bloody engagement. He replied to his signal officer: 'Leave off action! Now damn me if I do. You know I have only one eye. I have a right to be blind sometimes. I really did not see the signal.' As he said this he put his telescope to his blind eye. But blind-eyeing a signal from your boss to surrender on a point which you judge to be unnecessary is something entirely different from blind-eyeing an opponent's signal.

Ignoring a signal prolongs the argument. It is a stalling device that seldom comes off. It carries considerable risks of a breakdown because your opponent reacts negatively. Sometimes it works but make sure you are not simply rationalizing a failure on your part to pick up your opponent's signals.

Given a deadlock, and your willingness to negotiate a solution, you can break out of the argument by signalling or responding positively to signals sent by your opponent. Just introduce qualifications to your statements, for example, 'We do not *normally* give discounts', 'We cannot accept *all* of those changes', 'Your delivery schedules are *too* rigid'. These qualified statements should invite responses like: 'Under what circumstances would you consider giving a discount?', 'Which of the changes could you accept', 'How flexible do you require delivery schedules to be', etc. There is a fair chance that they will tell you.

From argument you have moved to proposals or the possibility of proposals. They may reply to your responses to their signals with a question of your intentions. For example, they may ask: 'Are you saying that you are prepared to consider our alternative proposals or amendments as a basis for negotiation?'. If you want to negotiate you will reply 'Yes', though you may qualify your answer with something like 'We are always prepared to consider reasonable suggestions for improving the acceptability of our proposals'.

Signalling behaviour does not make agreement inevitable, nor does it remove the conflict over the issues. It only makes negotiation about them possible and from this creates the possibility of agreement. We know of no way out of the argument step in a negotiation except by way of a signal.

The skilled negotiator will reward signalling behaviour where possible. By asking questions he will give the other side the opportunity to expand upon their qualifications to their opposition to whatever is being discussed. 'What do you mean by that?' is one form of putting a question following a signal. Or, 'By that we mean the following . . .' could be used by yourself to reinforce a signal you have given to the other side. You can also ask the other side for a proposal.

To be productive, signalling behaviour has to be reciprocated. Negotiators should require assurances before they move on anything; it is the only way they can move without surrendering. Handling concessions takes confidence and confidence can be strengthened by ensuring that any move you make will be followed by a move by the other side. We will discuss this more thoroughly in the chapters on proposing, packaging and bargaining but we can make a couple of useful points about ensuring mutual movement in the signalling step.

5.6   The ignored signal

What happens if you signal and there is no response from your opponent? The short answer is the argument step will continue. But you can do something about this yourself.

If a signal is ignored (or missed) you can repeat it, either verbatim or in another form. 'We cannot accept your position in its *current* form' can be repeated as 'You cannot expect us to accept your position in its *current* form'. If they have come to negotiate then sooner or later one of them will latch on to the word *current*. If they do not then you can improve the clarity of your signal by being a little more specific. You can tell them which specific items in their proposals give you the most difficulty in accepting. In doing so you will concentrate on the restrictive features (if you want to widen applicability) of their proposals. Again, if they have come to negotiate they will latch on to your signals. They might do this by asking you to justify your points of view.

However, if none of your signals are being picked up, you have the choice of sitting out the argument or withdrawing.

You can try one last form of signal if you decide to stay and that is by making an open and conditional signal. The signal may be as vague as you like, or as detailed as you like, but it must be a signal, *not* a concession. For example:

> 'Let us assume for the sake of the argument that we were to accept the principle behind your proposition, what assurances/discounts/delivery would you offer us in return?'
>
> *or*
>
> 'You have said repeatedly that our proposal is not acceptable. What amendments would we have to make to make it more acceptable to you?'
>
> *or*
>
> 'Without prejudice to the final outcome, or to the basic interests of each side, if we were to consider the points you have raised would you be prepared to consider our points?'

The answers to all of these questions, and the many more that can be devised for each situation, will do two main things. They will tell you whether the other party is willing to negotiate and, if so, what they are willing to negotiate about.

Having tried a signal, repeated it in different forms, made it more specific and presented it conditionally, and positively responded to any signals from the other side, you must be in a position either to move out of the argument or to decide whether negotiations are possible in current circumstances.

Deadlock is only inevitable if there is a refusal, an unwillingness, or an inability to negotiate and therefore a preference for some other solution to the conflict, such as the use of sanctions or the breaking-off of relations. Current circumstances may preclude successful negotiation. Time may have to pass before circumstances become propitious, perhaps by changing the personnel in each party, perhaps by modifying rigid attitudes. Time is often decisive in negotiations — if time did not matter there would be no point negotiating because if you can come to an agreement at any time agreeing now cannot be that important.

5.7 Checklist for signalling

- Are there any signs of *movement* in the argument?
- What signals have you made to indicate your own willingness to move?
- If they have been ignored, how can you reword them?
- What is the cause of his 'stonewalling'? Confidence or lack of it?
- Test his 'stonewalling' by a specific presentation of your signal linked to a specific call for him to reciprocate.
- If there is still no response you can:
  - *a* Break-off negotiations.
  - *b* Call upon him to seek authority to revise his position.
  - *c* Consider revising your own.
- Avoid making concessions in the 'hope' that he will respond — this only rewards intransigence.
- Listen for your opponent's use of non-absolute and qualified statements of his position, or references to his inhibitions.
- Ask him to elaborate on them. (His best move is to get your commitment to respond.)
- Respond positively, for example 'I am always prepared to consider reasonable suggestions for improving the acceptability of my proposals'.

- Memory joggers:
  Ignoring signals prolongs argument
  Listen more, talk less
  Respond and reciprocate
  Reward signals not intransigence

5.8 Common avoidable mistakes

- Not listening for signals
- Moving in response to intransigence
- Not exploring a signal
- Not reacting to a signal
- Not questioning a signal

6 Proposing

6.1 Introduction

Arguments, principles, opinions and prejudices cannot be negotiated, only propositions can, but propositions can be argued over. The way out of an argument is by a signal which leads to a proposition. In the negotiating context a proposition is an offer or claim which either establishes for the first time an opening position, or which moves away from an initial position. In many formal negotiations a great deal of debate may have taken place before a price or demand or claim is presented as an initial proposal. Subsequent proposals could be described as secondary proposals. However, the most common position in which we negotiate is not in a formal 'set piece' negotiation, but the minor conflicts of everyday life. We recognize these as negotiable conflicts because the parties state their ideal position:

'I want to have Friday off to visit the dentist.'

'But you can't have Friday off because I need you at my meeting.'

Any suggested compromise would be a secondary proposal. There are slightly different methods of handling primary and secondary proposals.

6.2 Agenda

A negotiation is not like cold-canvass selling; there is normally a recognized, if not agreed, issue or range of issues to be negotiated. Parties do not wander into a room and ask: 'What shall we negotiate about today?' They normally know why they are meeting and have some idea of the order of business, i.e. an agenda. This does not mean that the agenda cannot be changed — the order in which items are taken in a negotiation is sometimes of great importance.

Negotiation on the agenda can be a long and tiresome process. In the aftermath of the Falkland War Britain and Argentina had different views on what was negotiable. Argentina insists that sooner or later sovereignty over the Falklands must be discussed; Britain insists that only trade and air links are negotiable. Until a form of words is found that enables both parties to save face, the negotiations will concentrate on the agenda rather than the substance of their differences.

A party may declare that it has pre-conditions which must be met if it is to negotiate on some contentious issue. These pre-conditions are aimed at weakening the bargaining power of the opponent. For example, a union commonly insists that a dismissed employee be reinstated before they negotiate with the company over the substantive issues related to his dismissal. If the company agrees to this pre-condition it is giving up its main bargaining counter for securing concessions from the union on the related issues. The company wants to be able to say to the union: 'If you make concessions on these issues we will reinstate the employee, if you don't we won't'. The union's pre-conditions are aimed at preventing themselves being made to make that kind of choice.

Similarly, companies generally refuse to negotiate 'under duress'. They generally insist upon a return to normal working before they will negotiate with the union on a grievance. The union wants to use the strike, or go-slow, to be able to say to the company: 'If you make concessions and rectify our grievance we will return to normal working, if you don't we won't'.

Pre-conditions for negotiating can prevent negotiations

78

taking place until they are removed or modified. Whether they are removed or not will depend upon the balance of power between the parties, i.e. which side is hurt most by the *status quo* or the *status quo ante*.

6.3 Propose remedies

Negotiations might start off with a subject but they do not necessarily begin with two alternative propositions. The subject might be a claim for a 'substantial' wage increase, or an application for a renewal of a contract. What is meant precisely by 'substantial' and on what terms a contract would be renewed need not be specified at first. But at some point they would have to be.

It is imperative in grievance negotiations to become specific. Parties with a grievance are inclined to go on about whatever it is that has upset them, whether it is some disciplinary action that has been taken, or some disappointment they have experienced, or some failure they have noted in another party's performance. The result is, of course, an argument.

The skill of arguing is to get that step to work for your objective. The objective of somebody with a grievance is not merely to go over and over the grievance. The objective is to secure a remedy. Hence, *don't just state a grievance, propose a*

STEAK OUT

A diner complained to the waiter that he had ordered a medium rare steak but that he had been given a medium steak. The waiter replied that he had served a medium rare steak. They became locked in argument. The guest, pondering when the food would be eaten, suggested that the disputed steak be removed, that another one be cooked and, in the meantime, to compensate for the delay, a complimentary bottle of wine be served.

---

remedy. The remedy is your proposition. And there is a very high chance that attention will shift from circular argument about the grievance (who was to blame, etc.) to the proposed remedy.

We have all had experience of complaining about goods or services that have been faulty in some way. This is a common occurrence in restaurants, hotels, airline offices and stores. If you want to be convinced of the power of propositions over argument, the next time you have a complaint which is serious enough for you to make it known to whoever is supplying you, or not supplying you, with what you expected, think, before you approach them, what realistically do you want them to do about it? Tell them what you want them to do about it. It will work wonders. You may not get exactly what you demand first, but you will get something more than an apology in nine cases out of ten. By making a reasonable request for them to compensate for what they have done wrong you are giving them the opportunity to keep your goodwill. Most people will reply to such a request gladly. It gets them off the hook of trying to guess what they should do about your complaint.

If you are on the receiving end of a grievance, ask the person complaining what they want you to do about it. One third of them will have no remedy in mind and this cuts the argument short (especially if you apologize politely). Another third will suggest a remedy well inside your means. The final third will want something unreasonable or disproportionate to their grievance. With these people you can negotiate.

A proposition beats an argument. It gets things moving. It relieves tension caused by not knowing what it is the other side wants from you. Once you have their opening proposition you can concentrate on modifying it, if you need to, or considering it if you have to.

The opening proposals of one side in a negotiation may be on the table before the meeting. Unions sometimes send in written and detailed claims to the company before the annual negotiation. Naturally these are expected to represent their most ambitious position (their ideal). Some companies will have before them a detailed offer of a contract from a supplier and the negotiations will be about the possible terms for doing business. Just as often, the details may not be given of the union's claim or the offered contract, in which case the meeting will be about discussing the details. Each side will be trying to finesse out of the other the negotiating margin available.

Initial proposals are usually expressed firmly though their content is often vague:

'We demand a substantial increase.'

'I must get away early on Friday.'

'We insist on a tighter security policy.'

6.4 Proposal language

The initial proposal is usually a statement of a party's ideal position and the language used reflects the firmness of their position:

'I think we'd be looking for an earlier delivery.'

'I had hoped for an earlier delivery.'

'I must have delivery by Tuesday.'

By listening carefully to the language you can learn a good deal about their position.

MISREAD SIGNALS

The case of the employer who decided to short cut the traditional preliminary haggles by offering his top offer immediately only to find the men saying 'no', and demanding more, is well established in negotiating folklore. Why did it fail as a tactic? Because the men assumed that if the employer opened so high he must have even more to give. They revised their expectations. They moved their ideal further away from the employer than it was at the start. And why should they do otherwise? They had come to negotiate and he had come to settle quickly on his final terms. They misread his move and he misread their willingness to settle without a haggle.

A secondary proposal moves away from the clearly defined position. It feels the way forward to common ground. As a result it often appears to be tentative:

'Suppose we were prepared to . . .'

'I might be prepared to consider.'

The language used does not reflect a weakness but is a sign of caution and prudence.

'Are you saying', a negotiator might say to his opponent, 'that *if* we consider some relaxation of our position on this item, that you would drop your insistence on a penalty clause?' To which his opponent might (wisely and cautiously) reply: 'No, we would not drop the penalty clause but *if* your movement was great enough we would be prepared to *consider* modifying the penalty clause in *some* way'. Neither side have committed themselves and they must not do so until the details of the proposed 'relaxation' and proposed reciprocated 'modification' are known.

Tentative proposals reassure both sides. They help mark out the area from which agreement can eventually be achieved. They tell people what might be on offer if equally interesting concessions are made available by the other side.

6.5 Conditional proposals

In negotiation we are saying in effect that 'the position I open with is not the position I expect to end up with'. This is not the same as saying that 'any position other than the one I open with is acceptable to me'. The implication of negotiation is that there is the possibility of movement from an opening position but that there are also strong preferences to stick close to the opening position. After all you prefer your ideal to your limit position.

A proposal then, in this context, is a movement towards, if not into, the bargaining arena. Exchanging responses to tentative proposals coming out of the argument provides further information about each other's strengths of commitment to the issues in dispute. The parties 'stalk' around each other, trying to size up the possibilities.

Getting into the habit of making conditional propositions

is the best training for negotiating. If you start that way from the first proposal you make in a negotiation you will have no trouble coping with the bargaining stage where you need all the room for manoeuvre that is available. If you have thrown concessions away recklessly in the proposal stage — trying to 'buy peace' or 'get the sale' — you will only make life far more difficult for yourself later on.

Propositions are conditional: 'If you are prepared to do such and such, we are prepared to consider doing this and that'. (Note how you present your conditions first and make it specific — 'to do' not 'consider doing' — and how you make your part of the proposition tentative — 'consider doing'.)

They say in Yorkshire: 'You can't get owt for nowt' (obviously the cry of the negotiator). Nothing is for free in a negotiation. Everything is for exchange.

When stating a proposition it is a common technique to declare your ideal position and then immediately modify it — conditionally, of course. This can create the illusion of a concession where none has been made. A company may be seeking a ten per cent price increase and propose as follows: 'Under normal circumstances, it would now be necessary for

---

FROM SCENES LIKE THESE . . .*

'Would you be happier if we increased our offer?'

'Would you accept if we made it £40 instead of £38.50?'

'We have seriously considered your claims and decided to concede the following additional payments.'

'OK. We'll give you an extra £45. Is that all right?'

'Our revised offer is before you. Is it acceptable?'

'You've twisted my arm. They'll go bananas upstairs but if you will accept it, I'll give you a day off in lieu.'

'Let's make it £50. OK?'

. . . THEY GOT BAD BARGAINS!

* *All these were taken from actual negotiations.*

---

us to increase our price by 20 per cent from £100 to £120 per unit. However, in view of our excellent relationship, and on condition that you are prepared to continue buying from us, we are prepared to reduce this to £110.'

6.6 Firmness or flexibility?

Deciding exactly where to open is not an easy matter. It must be a highly subjective decision on your part though the following remarks should prove a useful guide.

First, consider the problem. You have to make a choice between firmness and flexibility, or rather some mixture of the two. The closer you remain to your original position the more firm your commitment; the further you are prepared to move away from it the more flexible your commitment.

Firmness can give you a negotiating platform for later flexibility. The higher your platform the more the opponent has to do to get you to agree to compromise. The danger is obvious. The firmer you are the higher the chances of a failure to agree on anything. Firmness can be taken as a sign that you are not willing to negotiate and your opponent may exercise the costly and disagreeable option of imposing sanctions to weaken your resolve and force flexibility upon you. He may simply decide not to do business with you at all. At the international level he may decide upon war as an alternative to your non-negotiable firmness.

On the other hand flexibility can remove all the negotiating cards you may be carrying. The more flexibility you display on every issue the more your opponent will conclude that you do not value your position very highly. What you do not value you do not fight for and he may simply increase his firmness in response to your boundless flexibility. This can clearly lead to exactly the same situation as over-firmness on your part, except this time it is you who is misreading his intentions.

Flexibility has a double advantage. It enables the negotiator to revise expectations upwards as well as downwards. If you have not been overly firm on a specific issue you may find it possible to revise your position in the light of your opponent's flexibility. Firmness on a general issue rather than a specific one is preferred at the opening of a negotiation — this gives you room to redefine what you mean as the positions, commitment and intentions of your opponent unfold.

For example, a firmly stated opening demand for a 'substantial wage increase' is a better negotiating position than an (opening) firm demand for '£280 a week'. Why? Because there is no less credibility in defining 'substantial' to mean '£280 a week' or some other figure less than this. The union leaders can declare a 'victory' or a 'success' on whatever they achieve and contain opposition from the militants who regard anything less than £280 as a 'sell out'. That is why militants try to commit union leaders to specific sums before they negotiate and why experienced union leaders resist such mandates, particularly when they believe that the militants, in order to undermine them as leaders in the eyes of disappointed members, are trying to commit them to totally unrealistic figures which are bound to be beyond attainment.

Public commitment to a specific figure is a useful way, however, of bringing maximum pressure to bear on the other party. If the union leaders agree to commit themselves to some figure they are, in certain circumstances, strengthening their negotiating position with the employers who see the publicity attached to the union's demands and are aware that a settlement well short of the publicized amount is going to be very difficult for the committed union leaders to accept. A similar tactic is regularly used in diplomatic negotiations. Government leaders make abrasive speeches on their country's demands, hoping to persuade the other party of how little room they have to move towards a compromise. This tactic often back-fires. Both countries adopt extreme public positions and deadlock ensues. This underlines the general point that deciding on an opening position and the associated tactics of displaying commitment to the other side is not easy.

Unions who get it right will settle higher than they otherwise would do. If they get it wrong the settlement may be delayed because their demands are unrealistic (well beyond the limit of the management). Sanctions may occur and the eventual settlement may mean a huge loss of face for one, or both, sides.

A broad rule suggests itself: be firm on generalities and flexible on specifics in the opening rounds. This gives you most room for manoeuvre. It follows that you should try to prevent your opponent being over-firm on specifics in the opening round if they are well outside your limit. You can avoid this to some extent by refraining from provoking him into an extreme position. Boxing him into a corner is not necessarily in your best interests — coming out of it may involve suffering damaging sanctions caused by his need to justify a retreat.

6.7 Realistic opening

We suggest as a general rule: '*Open realistically, move modestly*'. What is a realistic opening will depend a great deal on the circumstances of the negotiations and the environment normally associated with the type of negotiations you are engaged in.

In some negotiations there is a 'going rate' which other negotiations are settling at. Negotiations on wages, for example, often take place in a climate of precedent: what are other companies and unions settling at? The 'going rate' might be some notional figure such as the rate of inflation, or some target figure which the unions have taken as a norm. In commercial negotiations there may be some range of settlement normally accepted in that particular industry or between those particular partners. Also, the pressure of competition may force down an opening position below what it would be if the competition was not so apparent or so intense.

These kinds of considerations must be taken into account in your preparation and will help define a realistic ideal. Events can unfold which force a revision of the prepared positions, part of which could be the information discovered in the argument and signalling steps.

Choosing the opening position can be crucial. The tactic of disclosing the original ideal and justifying a move from it

COPY BOOK

Objective: purchase one photocopier, list price £6,500

Priorities: Like to get: £1500 discount
                 Intend to get: £1500 discount in non-cash form
                 Must get: £1000 discount in any form

Tradables: old copier for trade-in
                cash payment
                order today

Strategy: Take advantage of end of salesperson's quarter on Friday 12 September
                Enter showroom at 4.50 pm
                State intention to buy a copier immediately if they can meet a price of £5000

The negotiation:

'I need a price of £5000.'
'We could give you a discount of £900 for cash.'
'What trade-in can you offer for my old copier?'
'It's not really worth anything, but I can give you £200.'
'I'm prepared to take £200 in free copying.'
'I can only give you £150 on that.'
'If you include £75 of acetates, I might be interested.'
'Only if you sign the order immediately.'
'Unfortunately I cannot sign today without consulting may partner who wanted the old copier. But as it is not worth anything to you, why don't you give me the allowance, and let me dispose of it? Do that, and I can sign now.'
'OK.'
(The old photocopier was sold for £500 on Monday).

to an opening position has already been discussed. But a brief word about 'opening realistically' will serve a double purpose here: it will explain its meaning and identify its benefits.

People are educated by negotiations. The more regularly they negotiate with each other the more they learn about each other's styles. Not all negotiations are between people who know each other — some are single one-off negotiations. The parties may not meet again. Or the negotiation may be the first of a series.

Now the problem with all negotiations is the presence of uncertainty. You are not sure what the other side will settle for, you do not know about their style, you are not sure how to interpret what they say, you do not know how what you say affects your opponent, and therefore you need clues about the likely course of events once you get through the argument stage.

Consider the problem. When your opponent opens, is he beginning from a 'high' position but willing to move a lot, or is he only willing to move a little? Is the opening a genuine position? How serious is your opponent about his apparent willingness to accept a deadlock if his terms are not met? Is his firmness just caution or genuine commitment?

Uncertainty can be helpful to your position. Your opponent may interpret your stance as a definite commitment and try to bring you to a settlement by offering concessions quite out of step with your expectations.

Decreasing uncertainty in the negotiations may also help you. The more sure your opponent is of your commitment the more he can react rationally to your movements. If, for example, your negotiating style is known to be one in which you only move slightly off a declared position — once you have declared it — this enables the opponent to read your moves with a higher degree of accuracy and with less room for misinterpretation than if total uncertainty was present.

He will not, for example, assume that there is a wide range of alternative positions to which you might move if he argues or presses hard enough. His expectations, in other words, will remain bounded by your known negotiating behaviour. Unless you have totally misread the balance of power and the likely settlement range you will have structured your opponent's expectations in a range closer to his limit position than to yours.

On the other hand if you vary your style — sometimes open with a wide negotiating margin and sometimes with a narrow one — your opponent may misread the situation and assume the margin is wide when it is narrow. The aggravation that will ensue when your position becomes apparent will be quite damaging — people who feel 'betrayed', 'let down', 'misled' and so on will interpret your behaviour as 'intransigent', 'obstinate' and 'greedy'. You may face sanctions which were avoidable, or loss of business which was retainable. All because you contributed to misleading them.

A recent negotiation which led to a twelve-week stoppage gives an interesting example of this. The management opened the negotiations with an offer of 3 per cent, moved to 6 per cent and settled at 10 per cent. They will have great difficulty next year in selecting their opening position. If they open close to their limit they will face a major problem in convincing the unions that this is, in fact, close to their final offer and not one third of their final offer. If they open close to their most favourable position they will confirm the union's expectation and once again have long drawn out negotiations with the risk of industrial sanctions.

It is far better to open realistically, and to move modestly, than to open anywhere and move in large leaps sometimes

---

FLYING TOO HIGH

On a recent flight from Puerto Rico to New York, the plane was waiting to take off, when the flight attendant announced that the flight was 'oversold' and they wanted two volunteers to give up their seats. As an incentive he offered two free return trips from New York to the Caribbean. A stampede ensued, with a third of the cabin class passengers fighting to leave the plane. The flight left with 12 empty seats as the airline could not identify the first two volunteers. Was this an unrealistically high offer?

89

and smaller leaps the rest of the time. Act consistently. It pays you to 'educate' your opponents in your style and also in getting practice yourself in handling negotiations using the same tested methods. A determination to be realistic and make minor moves adds enormously to your confidence in presentation of your proposals. It will give you 'backbone' or what Londoners call 'bottle'.

Putting a proposal in an 'either-or' format is a very useful technique when dealing with uncertainty. 'We can quote you £505 for 12 weeks delivery CIF, or £423 for 16 weeks delivery FOB.' This type of proposal avoids instant acceptance or rejection. The other party might react strongly to one or other proposal. You receive information about whether it is price, delivery or contract type that is the problem.

The confidence with which you present a proposal is of great importance. The persons you are dealing with will be far more likely to know that you mean business than if you 'um' and 'ah' before getting to the point. Why does the car salesman have an advantage over the ordinary customer when negotiating a price for a particular car? First, he has more practice as he is doing the same thing several times a day with dozens of different customers, and second, he also has an advantage in the training he gets in being confident and precise. Whereas a customer who buys irregularly, perhaps once every two or three years, is less sure about how to ask for concessions and how to negotiate on the price. Being unsure about what to do, the inexperienced person is likely to be evasive and take a long time working up to a position, possibly via many reservations and qualifications. This is no problem for the car salesman. He always makes the opening offer (the numbers are two feet high on the windscreen) in order to structure your expectations. He will not offer concessions unless they are asked for and will only make a move when he thinks you have almost decided to buy.

In business negotiations you cannot rely on casual bidding. Indeed, as a business negotiator you are expected to act decisively and not to be embarrassed when acting in your company's interest.

CONFIDENCE COUNTS

Individuals discussing a possible sale of some second-hand item will go through the exchange of questions: 'What do you want for it?', followed by 'What will you offer?' Each person lacks confidence in presentation. Even then, statements such as 'My uncle bought one of them for £x', or 'My brother/wife told me not to spend more than £y', are likely to be made. Here they are putting the price decision on to somebody else, probably without justification. These kind of transactions might be concluded with the question: 'Would such and such be enough?' Here the person asking is trusting that the other person's good manners will restrain him from further haggling.

6.8 Presenting proposals

One way to improve your presentation of a proposal is to separate the proposal from its explanation and its justification. Itemize what is in the proposal first and then, if necessary, explain or justify its contents. Do not mix the two together otherwise the explanation or justification can sound very much like an apology. If it does and your opponent thinks you have doubts about it he must press you harder to get concessions. Your tone of voice and your mumbling meandering encourage resistance — they do *not* make it more acceptable.

A proposal in the form:

'If you can meet the following conditions: 1 . . . 2 . . . 3 . . . n . . . we will be prepared to consider offering the following: 1 . . . 2 . . . 3 . . . n. . . . Our reasons for doing so are a . . ., b . . ., c . . ., . . .'

is by far a more confident way of presenting something than the Shambolic Ramble Proposal style — if for no other reason than the more you explain a point the more opportunities you give your opponent to find something he disagrees with

91

in what you have said rather than what you have proposed. You also reveal your motivations which give away clues to your real commitments.

In presenting a proposal we are not advocating a stilted 'take-it-or-leave-it' presentation. Our point is that it is best to get the proposal with its conditions on the table *before* arguing for it. Of course, you might be able to identify possible alternatives to the items you are proposing but whether you digress while you are going through the items or after your exposition is a matter of personal style.

The best advice we can give when you are making a proposal is to state what you are proposing, if necessary why you are proposing specific items, and then to remain silent. The more you talk the more you reveal. Keeping quiet after your proposal puts pressure on both sides. If you interrupt your own silence, almost inevitably you will offer some additional concessions. Instead, keep quiet and let the pressure of the silence press on your opponent.

Having presented your proposal you are in the dominant position in the negotiation. You can use your proposal to gain a response: 'That is my proposal. Is it acceptable?' 'Why is it not acceptable?' or 'What would be acceptable?' Remember it is usually the first realistic, conditional proposal which lays the foundation of the final agreement. It seizes the initiative from the other party and forces the pace.

6.9 Receiving proposals

The other side of presenting a proposal is receiving one. Here we suggest two major rules.

Firstly, do not interrupt propositions. It never pays and sometimes it can cost a lot. If you interrupt a proposal you may miss something which was about to be proposed in addition to what you have already heard. People often tag on a concession at the end. An interruption may kill that concession completely. Interruption always antagonizes — nobody likes being interrupted — and one result is to cause bloody-mindedness in an opponent.

Secondly, do not engage in instant rejection. It seldom pays

THE SHAMBOLIC RAMBLE PROPOSAL STYLE

(*Paraphrased from a negotiation at a major processing plant in Scotland.*)

'We are prepared, as we always have been, though apparently it has not been made clear enough to you so far, to consult you about the use of contract labour, er, though we would have to think about what is the best arrangement, mutually, to carry out consultation — you know how difficult it is sometimes to get people together — God knows where they get to, sometimes it's like finding a needle in a hay stack — and we would have to work out something on the kind of notice we need from a production viewpoint — can't have plant on downtime — too much of that already — and I'm sure you want some notice to consult your people but don't start asking for money to do so — we have not got any. . . . Of course, we don't want you to think that we are using contract labour because we have no confidence in the maintenance section — why anybody should jump to that conclusion I don't know, it was never in our minds, and it was irresponsible for your officials to say it was. . . . We want you to know that our policy is only to use contract labour when we absolutely must, which is generally only when all the workforce in maintenance are working all the overtime there is around, so that aspect is up to you. If the men continue to work overtime as we need it we will not need to bring in so much contract labour, but we need notice and flexibility from your lads, we can't just turn on the tap at an hour's notice and get contractors — they have other companies to work for and we have to give proper notice, so we need notice from you if you are, or are not, willing to work overtime. There is too much sloppiness in the management of the overtime list; with all the changes it looks like a dog's breakfast — how anybody can read it beats me — this causes confusion and the inevitable complaints from your people and mine and I have to take time out when I can be doing other things to sort it out. So I do not see a problem if you agree to our proposals.'

off. Even when the proposition is absolutely unacceptable to you it is best to treat it, and the proposer, with some respect. You cannot be seen to be considering it seriously if you have rejected it out of hand. You may intend to reinforce your hard stance. But there are other ways of achieving the same ends which are less likely to antagonize your opponent. Everybody likes to have their views considered, so do not throw points away by screaming an instant 'no' when you do not have to.

Listen to the proposition. Ask questions to clarify any points you are not clear on (this may give you signal clues) and then either ask for time to consider it and adjourn or, if you are well prepared, give a considered response to it there and then.

A proposal deserves to be taken seriously as a proposal if not as a basis for settling the issue in dispute. If you have presented a proposal you will want a detailed response to it and indeed you should seek it even in the face of a blanket 'no' or other emotional outburst. A detailed response gives opportunities for signals.

You can answer which parts of the proposal are of interest to you for possible negotiation and which parts are not of interest. This tells your opponent what areas he has to work on. If you do not tell him this he is in the position of having made a proposal and not having information about what to do next. A blanket 'no' with no exposition is useless. It merely brings you back to the argument or even a breakdown.

When faced with a blanket 'no' you must ask for alternatives and try to coax them out of the other side. Saying 'no' is no basis for negotiation. You must not encourage people into saying 'no' by then rewarding them with your own alternatives every time they do so. Otherwise you will make all the movement and all the concessions and all they have to do is wait until they are sure you are squeezed dry and either say 'yes' or 'no'.

Your alternative proposal should take account of the progress of the negotiations up to that point. It should aim to find some common ground even if it is only a little. The tiniest common ground can be built upon. This does not mean that you will agree individually to items in their proposals at this stage — your best interests are served by keeping all issues linked, both those you agree with now and those they do not agree with yet. You should indicate areas where agreement might be possible provided the outstanding items can be settled. This edges the negotiations away from the opening exchanges of proposals towards the packaging step.

The most useful technique in handling proposals and counter-proposals is that of summarizing — this keeps people's minds concentrated. Summaries organize the business before the meeting, remind everybody of what is going on and demonstrate that you are listening attentively to the other side.

We have referred to the 'balance of power' in negotiation. This balance is changed by proposals. The person who has just made a proposal can get into a strong position. He can adopt the attitude: 'I have made you a proposal, if you do not like it, what is your alternative?' Even if his proposal has received a flat rejection he can repeat this question. He passes responsibility for the next stage firmly to the other side.

6.10 Adjournments

A word on adjournments. The number and frequency of adjournments will depend upon the normal practice of negotiators in the environment in which they are operating. Employee negotiations might adjourn more frequently than commercial negotiations but not always. A major contract negotiation may be spread, of necessity, over many meetings.

The main purpose of an adjournment is to review and assess progress against the prepared objectives of yourself and your estimates of your opponent's objectives. They give an opportunity to up-date your strategy against what you and your team have witnessed. This cannot be stressed too much; adjournments are partially repreparation sessions for the reconvened meeting. The L-I-M objectives can be reconsidered in the light of information gleaned at the negotiations.

If the adjournment is taken to consider a specific proposal rather than being a natural break, i.e. for food or sleep, or a weekend, it is important to bear in mind that adjournments

THE ORDERED SEQUENCE PROPOSAL STYLE

'If you are prepared to meet the following conditions:
1   Your availability for consultation with reasonable notice.
2   A guarantee that the workforce will make a minimum number of themselves available for overtime working.
3   Adequate notice of unavailability for overtime working by each employee.
we would be prepared to consider offering the following:
1   Consultation between the maintenance manager and the stewards on his intentions to use contract labour on a specific project.
2   Agreement that contract labour would only be used if the project cannot be covered by normal and overtime working using our own labour.
3   A statement re-affirming our continued confidence in our own labour's performance in the maintenance department.'

If necessary, or if asked to do so, the reasoning behind the propositions could be given but once again in a 1,2,3 format, sticking tightly to the conditions and the proposals.

under these conditions create expectations of a response in the minds of the opposition. Reading what is going on is vital and keeping your mind on your objectives is an essential part of that.

A wrongly timed adjournment can actually weaken the pressure upon the opposition. By the time they reconvene they have got a second wind or new instructions. In commercial life an adjournment can let the competition in: while you are considering how to reject the offer before you, your rivals have gone in and sewn up the deal.

Remember secondary proposals are tentative and exploratory in the opening rounds. They are suggestions. They point the way the negotiation may proceed. They are the storecupboard of ingredients which you will later use to prepare the final dish.

Do not reject the menu on the grounds that one dish is not to your liking. When compiling your menu offer as many choices as possible for each course.

It will create a more productive and positive atmosphere if you agree 'to consider', or to 'to investigate' items in a proposal although you might reject them outright at a later stage.

The more variables you can introduce in the opening steps the better chance of an agreement which satisfies both parties.

The next steps are the more intensive aspects of the negotiating process: packaging and bargaining. These skills require the most attention and the most practice by negotiators. This is where the money is earned, where the prizes are won and where the most satisfaction is to be gained. Everything so far has been leading up to these two steps.

6.11 Checklist for proposing

- Propositions overcome arguments because arguments cannot be negotiated.
- Proposals advance negotiations.
- Proposals seize the initiative.
- Unrealistic proposals prolong arguments.
- Interrupting proposals provokes arguments.
- Secondary proposals are best put as suggestions.
- Proposals must address the needs of the parties.
- Proposals can be used to gain responses.
- Be firm on generalities, e.g. 'We *must* have compensation.'
- Be flexible on specifics, e.g. 'We *propose* £10,000 compensation.'
- Do not use weak language, e.g. 'We hope', 'We like', 'We prefer'. Use strong language, e.g. 'We need', 'We must have', 'We require'.

- State your conditions first and be specific.
- Follow with your proposition and be tentative.
- Opening concessions should be small rather than large.
- Opening conditions should be large rather than small.

- Memory joggers:
  Don't just state a grievance, propose a remedy
  Open realistically
  Move modestly
  Invite a response

6.12 Common avoidable mistakes

- Complaining but not proposing
- Using 'weak' language: 'I'd like', 'We wish'
- Making unconditional proposals
- Negotiating with yourself before you meet the other side
- Opening with an unrealistic offer
- Behaving inconsistently in moving your positions
- Smothering a proposal in verbage
- Interrupting a proposal
- Taking an opponent's proposal to be set in concrete instead of being open to negotiation

7   Packaging

7.1   Introduction

Packaging moves the negotiations into the bargaining arena. It is the antechamber of the bargaining step, the bridge between the opening movements and the final coming together of the negotiators. It is, effectively, activity which draws up the agenda for the bargaining session.

Before we consider the packaging step let us review the progress of a hypothetical negotiation up to this point.

The parties have prepared well. They have defined their objectives and graded them in order of priority. The argument has revealed new information and some of the attitudes, interests and inhibitions of the other side. If they have been watching and listening they will have recognized the signals showing that a negotiated settlement is possible and desirable. By a series of proposals and counter-proposals the principal variables have been mapped out.

Now the time is right for packaging.

7.2   What is a package?

Negotiators sometimes open with what they call a 'package' of proposals. This is not what we mean by packaging. An opening 'package' is simply a set of proposals which the negotiator presents without considering what the other party wants. Packaging, as we mean it, is a considered activity in response to the opening moves of the negotiation. It is purposive — it aims to facilitate mutual progress from where the parties are to where they might settle. It differs therefore from a list of opening demands or offers because the purpose of those kind of 'packages' is to set out their proposer's objectives, not their revised objectives in response to their opponent's reactions.

The beauty of packaging is that in total a package will present the variables in a form which more closely matches the other party's interests and inhibitions — indeed, a package may withdraw concessions previously granted and substitute less costly items if the overall result is likely to be more attractive to the other party.

7.3 Rules

The rules for packaging are:
1   Address your package to the interests and inhibitions of the other party.
2   Think creatively about all the possible variables.
3   Value your concessions in the other party's terms.
Your perception of the other party's interest may be different from their perception of the other party's interest may be different from their perception of their own interests. Packaging enables you to influence them, perhaps enough to alter their perceptions. You might say to them:

> 'If we were to meet you on this wage claim we would have to de-man the operation by 20 per cent.'

or:

> 'If we were to meet that quality specification we would have to delay delivery by up to six months.'

or:

> 'If you go to the Club tonight I cannot guarantee I shall still be here when you come home.'

You are showing them the consequences of their insistence

on a course of action. This can be followed by a package which meets their interests:

> 'However, we could afford a substantial pay increase in return for higher productivity.'

> 'However, if you are prepared to cover the higher cost we could achieve the higher specification and meet your delivery deadline.'

> 'If you promise to take me to dinner next week, I'll let you go to the Club without me tonight.'

Parties who reject your proposal need not be plain awkward

REMEMBER THEIR INHIBITIONS

An aircraft manufacturing company wanted to introduce a new production bonus scheme to increase output and replace the current payment system. Considerably increased earnings were available to encourage worker acceptance. Opposition was voiced by the union representatives — a major feature being loss of jobs. To overcome the opposition, the company negotiators increased the offer of higher wages and substantial numbers of employees were attracted by the new bonus proposals.

In order to clinch the deal, the company stated that future job security could be threatened unless full acceptance was agreed. In subsequent ballots the proposals were decisively rejected.

Negotiators must package their proposals in ways which are sensitive and understanding of the inhibitions preventing the other side from reaching agreement. In this case there was a genuine and widespread fear of job losses and the company's final package and accompanying threat simply increased those fears. In this way failure was snatched from the jaws of success.

---

or bloody-minded. It may be that your proposal does not (yet) address their needs, and, instead threatens their inhibitions. If your proposal is aimed at the wrong target, then increasing your offer is not going to make it more attractive.

7.4 Variables and tradables

Not every situation can be resolved by negotiation, but many which appear to be insoluble are deadlocked only because of a lack of creativity in using variables as tradables. Issues are not self-contained entities. They have dimensions (how much?), destinations (who gets them?), timing (when?) and conditions (price?). These are variables. It is the variables that are traded: a little more of this, a little less of that. Much of the skill of packaging lies in the ability to open up new variables for trading. Instead of being stuck along one dimension — a higher price for me means a lower price for you — we try to introduce new variables to trade for movement on the price. Hence, what I might lose on price, I could be prepared to accept if I got something on delivery, or quantity, or when I get paid. Naturally the more issues available in packaging the more flexibility there is for the packager.

There is considerable scope for creating variables if you look for them. Money produces many variables: stepped increases, shared costs, extended credit, fixed charges, variable charges, penalty clauses, compensation clauses, interest rates, denominated currencies and so on.

To help you think creatively about packaging ask yourself this question about any issue:

'WHO gets HOW MUCH of WHAT WHEN?'

There will not always be an answer to every part of the question but it should trigger off some thoughts about possible variables. Packaging involves actively seeking variables and these are not always obvious. This is one of the reasons why we advocate that you keep as many options open from the earlier rounds of the negotiations by refraining from agreeing separately to issues. Keep everything linked if you can, it will give you more scope in the packaging and bargaining steps.

```
TIME AS A TRADABLE

Long Time
The lease on this land (and anything built on it)
will revert to the freeholder after 999 years.

Elastic Time
A manager wishing to rent a car from 10am to be
returned at 1pm the following day agrees to forego
the 15 per cent discount if the hire company agreed
to a 27 hour day.
```

It is best for you that you discover the variables open
to you and do not rely on your opponent's 'goodwill and
generosity'. It may be in his interest to sit still and watch you
struggle to avoid having to make a concession and get nothing
in return. It is rarely the case that an opponent will say to
you: 'Seeing you have been so generous to me, I will give you
the following . . .'. If you have already conceded the low-
value side-issues (from your point of view) you have nothing
to use at the very moment when you need them most. What
is of low value in general terms may have a very high value
when you desperately need some movement from your
opponent.

7.5   What is it worth?

While negotiation is about movement it is our view that the
early steps of a negotiation require indication of a willingness
to move and not necessarily an actual movement. In other
words a signal that movement is possible is not the same
as an actual concession. Some negotiators disagree and are
prepared to demonstrate their willingness to move by
releasing some minor concessions early on in the negotiation
to 'oil the slope' to a compromise. They believe that this
creates 'goodwill'.

We do not reject this view out of hand — negotiating is a
matter of personal style and circumstance — but we are

ADDRESS THE INHIBITIONS!

A group made a take-over bid for a small company which had been built up by an entrepreneur. The offer was refused as were two subsequent offers. The group were at a loss to understand why this was. They failed to uncover the real inhibitions of the entrepreneur.

As a man of 40, comfortably off and the unchallenged boss of his company he had little need for cash. His concerns were: 'How could I operate within a large group and, if I left, what would I do for the next 25 years?'

The owner eventually sold out for a smaller sum to a group who offered to put him in charge of a new venture with complete operating autonomy plus a seat on the main board.

If the other party is not responding to your concessions maybe it is because you are not addressing his inhibitions?

HOW MUCH IS ENOUGH?

If you want someone to accept something which is unpalatable to them in principle, you can suggest a long lead time before its introduction. Then when you have agreed the principle, you negotiate on the length of the lead time. You can use the same device of separating principle from consequence where the variable is not time but money.

George Bernard Shaw illustrated this in his famous example of the high-born snooty woman and the seducer. The man asked if she would sleep with someone for £500 to which she replied: 'Possibly'. He then asked her to sleep with him for £5. She replied, indignantly, 'What do you think I am, a whore?' The man replied: 'We have already established what you are, we are just haggling over the price'.

sceptical of its generality. Signs of movement are needed and if minor concessions are to be made they must in our view follow the basic rule of exchange — 'you move on that and we will move on this' — and not become free gifts. Goodwill is a two-way street and exchanging small movement is a sounder policy than living in hope with one-way gestures.

Telling your opponent what is on offer — the package — and being ready to exchange concessions, large and minor, is the strongest negotiating platform you can build. It prepares the way to the bargaining step where the exchange will take place. Early exchanges are in order; we only have reservations about early 'free gifts' because they narrow your negotiating room.

A common failing amongst negotiators is to ignore the other party's perceptions. They offer concessions without considering what their value is to the other party. Worse still, they sometimes give concessions without even realizing that they have done so. They look at an item as minor, irrelevant requests to be agreed and brushed aside in their headlong dash in pursuit of what they regard to be the 'nub' of the issue.

Any request, no matter how insignificant should be looked upon as an opportunity to trade.

Having conceded several minor points early on with the

A MISSED TRADE

Customer: 'We'd like you to give a key note address to our national conference in June. We like to hear a supplier's views on perspective changes in our energy policies.'

Supplier: 'I am sure my managing director would be pleased to speak for you. On this other matter, have you been able to persuade your finance department to accept our direct debiting scheme?'

Customer: 'I'm afraid not.'

---

substantive issues left outstanding, you often find that your opponent increases his hostility levels because of your alleged intransigence. The early concessions are forgotten and will certainly be played down. But if you still had them to deploy you might be able to make a much more attractive package with some concessions on the main issues plus some other concessions on the (to you) minor issues.

Everything you are asked for in a negotiation is requested by the opposition because it is worth something to them. Even information can have value. What is of minor consequence to you may have immense value to the other party. Therefore you must value the concessions in the other party's terms, not just your own.

Ask yourself three questions before trading a concession:

1   What is the concession worth to my opponent?
2   What does it cost me?
3   What do I want in exchange?

No matter how low the value of the concession to you, if it has value to your opponent get it to work for your negotiating objective.

This is all the more essential when an opponent asks you

CHEERS!

A company using a group of rooms in a hotel for a training course used two unused bedrooms which were converted for syndicate sessions. On the last night of the course the hotel manager asked the course organizer if he could help him out with a problem which had arisen from over-booking by reception. He needed the two bedrooms that night for guests who were arriving in an hour's time. The course trainer agreed because he had finished with the syndicate/bedrooms. The concession for him therefore had a nil cost. However, he agreed to relinquish the use of the rooms on condition that the management of the hotel provided a champagne lunch for the course delegates. The result was one happy course and one happy manager.

---

for something which unbeknown to him you were intending to offer anyway. There is a great temptation to concede it quickly and sometimes entirely unconnected to the flow of the negotiations. It is simply thrown away. But a packager will hold on to these kinds of concessions and work them into the package. He will present this kind of concession (already budgeted for) as a tradable, not a throw-away.

7.6 L-I-M again

The package addresses itself to some, perhaps all, of the interests and inhibitions of the other side. How far an opponent's interests are taken into account will depend upon the intensity of the conflict, the balance of forces and the best interests of your own side. The LIKE TO GET/INTEND TO GET/MUST GET framework used in your preparation will assist you in preparing a package.

Having categorized your objectives in this format you have available to yourself both the possibility and the means of movement, if circumstances dictate that movement is necessary to achieve a settlement.

You can use your LIKE TO GET proposals as concessions in the bargaining session and you can set this up by repackaging them in your new proposals.

Because they are your most ambitious proposals and, by definition, may be sacrificed, you have the greatest room to manoeuvre in redrafting them as variables in your package. Of course, it may be that the negotiations have shown that you can make progress on the LIKE TO GET items, or because they are ambitious, that you can use them by extending them a little, as 'frighteners' to move your opponent closer to you on your MUST and INTEND items.

The package leads the negotiations to the bargaining arena and therefore it must contain items that can be modified or exchanged as bargains with the other side. This is why you do not necessarily strip your opening proposals completely of everything that is unacceptable to your opponent. Let him bargain them away from you by concessions on his part. It is permissible to modify a proposal in the package, or to

DON'T CALL ON ME, I'LL CALL ON YOU

Following an unsatisfactory stay at a London hotel a businessman listed his grievances to the management and also proposed what remedies he required from them. On his return to Scotland he received a telephone call from the UK sales director of the hotel chain. The director offered to fly up to Scotland to apologize in person for the hotel's failings which badly affected the businessman's marketing promotion. That was the director's proposal.

The businessman counter-proposed by re-packaging the director's proposal: 'Send me a return air ticket and I will fly down to London and you can apologize to me there'. This was accepted.

Its acceptance was based on both parties achieving their objectives. The sales director saved time and effort and had the advantage of offering his apology in his own office, where he was also in charge of the hospitality. The businessman was able to undo some of the commercial damage done to his marketing presentation by the hotel and gained the cost of a business trip to London which he had been planning anyway.

extend another item if you are compelled by circumstance to drop something. The more you have available for exchange in the bargaining session the better it is for you, and your chances of getting a settlement.

7.7 Checklist for packaging

- Identify your opponent's inhibitions, objectives, their priorities, and the signalled possibilities of concessions.
- Review your opponent's and your own objectives in the light of L-I-M.

'WELLY BOOTS'

The scene was a major wage negotiation. The union had presented the normal shopping list of claims covering many and varied demands for improvements in this rate, that bonus, that allowance and so on.

Amongst the 21 points appeared a claim for a free issue of 'welly boots' to employees.

The company negotiators rejected this item at an early stage. It reappeared, after every adjournment, in the union's restated claims. The company side was astonished. Their own assessment had suggested that this was a 'like to get' makeweight and the union would not press it. After many adjournments, the majority of the company team were weakening and advocated concession on the boots issue in order to make progress in the negotiations. The principal company negotiator disagreed and following the next adjournment finally rejected the 'welly boots' item. The trade union leader, in reply, noted the rejection with the comment 'we had all forgotten who raised it in the first place'.

If you have prepared well, listened to the signals and analyzed the opposition's priority objectives, do not be deflected by red herrings.

- Is there enough movement indicated to produce a package?
- How can you address your package to meet some/all of your opponent's inhibitions?
- What concessions are you looking for?
- What negotiating room do you have in your current positions?
- Which concessions are you going to signal in the package?

- What do you want in return?
- How equitable is the concession rate?
- Draw up your list of conditions and place them in front of your package.
- Have you considered *all* the possible *variables* in the package? Can you create some new variables in any aspect of your relationship with your opponent and introduce them as tradables?

- Memory joggers:
    Who gets how much of what when?
    Address the inhibitions
    If it's valued it's variable
    Value your concessions in the other party's terms

7.8 Common avoidable mistakes

- Not addressing the inhibitions
- Carelessly exciting their inhibitions
- Limiting oneself to a single variable
- Not seeking new variables
- Not valuing variables in the other party's terms

8 Bargaining

8.1 Introduction

Bargaining is about exchanging — something gained for
something given up. It is the most intense part of the negotiating process and both parties have to pay close attention
to what they are doing. Ill-judged concessions by one party
can make the difference between a successful (profitable)
outcome and a less successful, and possibly unprofitable,
outcome. In this chapter we will outline some simple techniques by which a negotiator can ensure that the outcome is
favourable to his interests.

8.2 The big IF

The most important single rule for the bargaining step is to
make all propositions and concessions, indeed practically any
statement at all, *conditional*. Nothing, absolutely nothing, is
given away free. Everything, absolutely everything, is
conceded in exchange for something else.

We call this the big IF.

'If you agree to X, I will agree to Y.'

The key word is 'IF'. Placing an 'IF' in front of a statement
protects it from being misappropriated by your opponent.
Without an 'IF' he can simply say 'Thank you very much'
and pocket your concession without reciprocating. And

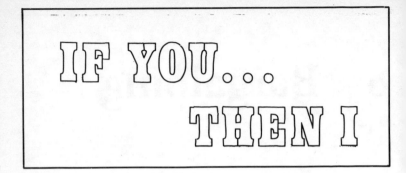

IF YOU...
THEN I

most times that is precisely what he is invited to do by inexperienced negotiators who for some reason assume that if they are generous to their opponents they will eventually persuade them to be generous in return. What is more, many negotiators, despite the evidence of experience, continue to try the generosity gambit and fail to see the connection between their failures as negotiators and their behaviour as the bestowers of free gifts.

Start using 'IF' and see the difference. Two things will happen. First, your opponent will receive a clear signal from you about the price you place on a concession. Second, you will educate him in bargaining behaviour: all concessions from you must be paid for by concessions from him.

If you do not educate him in bargaining behaviour he will naturally assume that concessions from you are his by right or might. Neither assumption is to your advantage. Negotiating then becomes a process of surrendering to his ideal position. You have to settle for less than you need to. You can rationalize this by taking consolation from the fact that you 'bought peace' ('at least they did not strike') or you 'got the order' ('a full discount order is better than no order'). But as rationalizations they are poor substitutes for winning agreements closer to your ideal than to his.

This is particularly true when the remedy is to use a single two-letter word.

Instead of saying 'OK. We will concede this point. Now will you agree?' (often not even the last point is said!), you should present it as: 'IF you agree to the package now, *then* we will modify our position on this point'. You have not

112

conceded the point in dispute because of the presence of 'IF'. There is, if you like, an invisible piece of string tied to the offered concession which you pull back if they do not agree to your concession.

If your opponent answers 'Yes' to your condition, you have an agreement. If he says he has other points of difference which must be settled before he can agree to the package, you simply respond by asking him to state the differences in full, being careful not to make any concessions in isolation.

You should note that there are different ways of using bargaining language, not all of them helpful. Consider the sentence: 'If I agree to your request, then will you agree to mine?' This uses 'If . . . then' but it is not a proper bargaining offer. It is in fact a question, which experience shows is often followed by a 'no'.

Bargaining proposals should be statements not questions: 'If you confirm the discount, and deliver in seven days, then I will process the order'. Statements tell the other party the price of agreement. They do not ask a closed question that invites a 'no', or a continued haggle. Hence, remember to make your bargaining proposal in the form of 'If you . . . then I'.

The big IF is a defensive shield round your offers of concessions. It is your price tag. If he does not like your price it is up to him to tell you and for you to make clear how firm your price is or what alternative prices you will consider accepting. Unless and until he meets your price you will not give him a concession. You give nothing on account. Nothing for goodwill. Nothing on trust. Everything is priced in the bargaining step. True you are always open to offers. But offers are not based on right or might — they must be something that you want for whatever it is you are being asked to give.

8.3 Leading with conditions

Some negotiators 'forget' to put their conditions on their concessions. They are so concerned with getting their revised offer right and with getting it across to the opponent, before

IF YOU . . . THEN

Examples of the moves in a bargaining session are illustrated in the following example. (We have only reproduced the actual moves and have edited out the 'verbiage', some of it of a long duration, which separated the moves from each other.)

Mgt: If you agree to drop the claims for meal allowances, shift payment improvements and increased holidays, then we are prepared to make an improved offer on basic rates of pay.

Union: We would be prepared to consider dropping these items but this would be dependent upon the size of your offer on basic rates . . . (*adjournment*).

Mgt: If you confirm your willingness to remove these items from the table, then we will improve our offer from 10 to 12 per cent.

Union: That proposal is not acceptable. However, if you would be prepared to consider an increase to 15 per cent then we might be in a position to reach some accommodation with you . . . (*adjournment*).

Mgt: We cannot accept your proposal. However, in an attempt to reach final agreement with you we would be prepared to improve our last position on condition that your side unanimously recommended acceptance of the total package; that the agreement would have a duration of 12 months and you were able to accept the additional payment 3 months after the implementation of the deal.

Union: We accept a 12 months duration and do not disagree in principle to a two-stage payment. We will certainly recommend acceptance *if* your second stage payment is acceptable to us.

Mgt: In that case our final offer is as follows. On condition that all other items are now dropped; that the agreement will have a duration of 12 months and that the trade union recommends acceptance of the total deal, then we will pay a 12 per cent increase in basic rates now and a further 2 per cent in 3 months' time.

Union: We agree.

they are interrupted, that they forget to place conditions upon it. Sometimes they remember a few minutes later and try to introduce their conditions as a desperate afterthought. It is not always easy to get conditions onto the table *after* the concession has been offered because your opponent reacts to this negatively. Either he does not take the condition seriously — he has already pocketed the concession mentally — or he treats the attempt as a breach of convention — he thinks you are trying to up the *ante* out of turn.

The best way to avoid this situation is to always lead with your conditions. Get them up front. Then tell them what you will give to them if they accept what you have stated as your condition.

'If you agree to X, we will agree to Y'; 'Provided that you accept X, we will agree to Y'; 'On condition that you do X, we will do Y'. And so on. Each form of presenting a concession has the conditions stated first.

Note also how the bargaining offer is presented: the condition and offer are specific. 'If you agree/you accept/you do' then, and only then, will 'I' agree to do something for you. Tell him what *he* must do, to get you to do something for him. If he says 'Yes', you have agreement; if he says 'No' you can modify your position or require that he does so.

115

You may need room. He may agree to some modified version of your condition. In which case you are able to modify your concession. For example, you might say something like: 'If you agree to six-man crews, we will increase the shift premium payment'.

Their best answer is to ask you by how much you will raise the payment. This sets a bottom limit on the reward for agreeing with you. You can reply that conditional upon them agreeing to six-man crews you would consider paying up to £X a shift, choosing a figure below your top price. Now they can come back and argue for more money or argue for larger crews. You have retained the flexibility to move on either the money or the crew-size because your initial offer was conditional. If they insist on eight-man crews, you can move downwards on the shift premium quite legitimately because your offer was conditional on the six-man crew. If they move upwards on the money demand and crew size you are able to repackage either more men for the same money, or more money for the same men. You may even move on both variables.

The one thing you will not do is agree on one variable

(AND AGAIN!)

Discipline cases involving sackings are a major cause of industrial disputes. It must not be forgotten that the MUST GET objective is to improve future behaviour by establishing agreed rules of conduct and thereby avoid the recurrence of similar problems.

The solution to the immediate issue of punishment for the individual concerned is only relevant in negotiations when it recognizes the priority of objectives. Therefore a legitimate bargaining position in a sacking case might be: 'If you agree that all future offences of this nature will be treated as dismissal cases, then on this occasion we will give the employee one more chance'.

---

without the other. To agree on crew size first and then on the money is courting an expensive error, assuming these are the only two variables in contention. The conditionality of the offer compels the other side to bargain by giving something up to get something it wants.

It is usual and safer in the proposal step to make tentative offers: 'I will consider', 'I will look into', 'perhaps', 'possibly' and so on. In the bargaining step you will firm up your proposals and become more positive: 'If you will do X, I will do Y'.

It is sometimes useful to encourage the continuity of the bargaining step by using such expressions as:

'I feel we have the elements of an agreement here. . . .'

'We have made significant progress although a number of issues still separate us. . . .'

'Given the measure of agreement we have achieved it would be a great pity to allow the negotiations to founder on the remaining issues. . . .'

8.4 Link the issues

It is a common strategy in negotiation to present a list of demands, objections, requirements, etc., followed by the 'logical' suggestion that they are dealt with one at a time.

You must never let yourself fall for this trap if you are the party expected to respond to the list. It is essential to keep all the issues in dispute linked up to the bargaining step.

If you negotiate piecemeal you will get chopped up. Your opponent may be delighted if you negotiate each item on an individual basis. That way he can squeeze you. To get agreement on one item you will make concessions. This uses up your negotiating capital and might exhaust it before you get agreement on all the issues that are outstanding. Then you face a real problem. You have nothing more to concede and you are still short of an agreement.

This leaves you with two very different alternatives. You can give up hope of getting an agreement and suffer whatever

KEEP THEM LINKED

A golf club wished to make certain alterations to the clubhouse to accommodate some gaming machines. The only available space was in part of the professional's shop. The professional paid no rent for his shop but he did have a contract with the club which had two years to run. The professional sensing an opportunity to *(a)* enjoy a share of the profits from the gaming machines, *(b)* improve his present terms of contract and *(c)* renew his contract for a further period, submitted a list of demands.

The demands included alternative storage space, sales facilities in other areas of the clubhouse, improved access, a stronger voice on the management committee, a new contract and annual compensation of £3,000 for his alleged loss of sales from his loss of space in the shop.

Many of these items cost the club very little and they conceded them early on without linking them together to the demands they did not want. In particular the professional continued to press for £3,000 compensation. This was totally unacceptable to the club committee.

After several fruitless attempts to make the professional change his mind the committee intimated that it was dropping the gaming machine idea and therefore would revert to the existing arrangement with the professional.

The professional's attitude changed. He decided that having achieved two of his objectives, *(b)* and *(c)*, he was prepared to drop the other *(a)*. The position was now reversed with the professional trying to persuade the committee to go ahead with the machine plan. Eventually the committee agreed but this time linked everything together. They were also able to claw back their earlier commitment on *(b)* without any concessions on *(a)*.

A DEAL IS A DEAL

A young man offered to buy a field off a farmer to use for his car auction business. The agreed price was £600 (in 1946!). It took some months to raise the cash. Meanwhile, the farmer changed his mind. He demanded £1000. They haggled and eventually agreed on £800.

The young man was furious at this pressure tactic. He eventually raised the extra cash and handed it over. When the papers were signed, he thumped the farmer on the nose for going back on the original bargain.

Years later, the young man, now a multi-millionaire, sold the same field for £7.5 million. He did not get rich by cheating on his deals.

this costs you. Or you seek new authority to extend your concessions and take the inevitable criticism from your principals. Salesmen are taught how to 'handle' buyer objections by 'overcoming them'. In practice this means conceding on each objection until the buyer runs out of objections or the seller runs out of concessions.

If you link the issues by agreeing to 'consider that', 'think about this' and so on until all the items are listed which the other party wishes to raise then you can deal with them within your total package: agreement on one is conditional upon agreement on them all. The packaging step should have given you the opportunity to set the link up, the bargaining step can then utilize the linked issues to secure the distribution of your negotiating capital across all the issues in dispute. A movement here is compensated by a movement there. A concession on item A is linked to a small concession on item B and two large concessions on items C and D.

This way the negotiator is not picked off piecemeal. Any offered concession on one item is conditional upon agreement on the other outstanding items. If pressure is put on you to concede more on a subsequent item than you had planned then it is possible for you to replay the previously offered

---

ARMS CONTROL AND 'SPIES'

Soviet–US relations began to thaw with the coming to power of General Secretary, Gorbachov, and the first summit he held with President Reagan in 1985. The second summit was placed in jeopardy by the activities of alleged spies. A Soviet employee at the United Nations was arrested by the Americans on charges of spying, and twenty-five other Soviet citizens were listed for deportation, suspected of similar activities. Meanwhile, an American journalist was arrested in Moscow charged with 'spying for the CIA'.

President Reagan linked the case of the American journalist to progress towards arranging the second summit. Implication: release the journalist or a less productive summit. The Soviet response was to link the arrested UN official, and the 25 others threatened with deportation, to the second summit. Implication: release our citizens, or no release of the journalist and no progress at the second summit.

The Americans protested that there was no comparability between the cases; the Soviets insisted that there was, and threatened retaliatory deportations of US citizens in Moscow to match any carried out in New York. Linking the issues of the 'spies' to the second summit threatened both normal relations and the prospects for arms control.

---

exchange on an earlier linked item and require that it is amended if the other party insist upon you giving way on the subsequent item. All items are negotiated conditionally upon the package as a whole being agreed. Each side reserves the right to revise an earlier conditional concession in the light of subsequent discussions.

The strength of treating the issues as a package lies in maintaining the links between the issues. Allow one issue to slip out from the package and you weaken the package as a whole. It will cost you more that way. Keep them linked and you keep them for trading. The more items you have to trade in the bargaining stage the stronger your position.

You must choose whether to link issues or not, and how to link them if you decide it is to your advantage. Sometimes it is not to your advantage. Sometimes it is unrealistic for you to try to do so.

Hence, linking must be realistic. You must think about linking issues in the bargaining step if it is realistic and to your advantage for you to do so. In most cases it is. It is better to attempt to link the issues than to forego the added flexibility it will give you. In a tight negotiation you need all the room for manoeuvre you can get.

8.5   Checklist for bargaining

- Absolutely firm rule — no exceptions at all, ever:

    EVERYTHING MUST BE CONDITIONAL

- Decide what you require in exchange for your concessions.
- List and place that at the front of your presentation.
- Signal what is possible if, and only if, they agree to your conditions.
- If the signal is reciprocated present your proposals, re-stating your conditions.
- Keep all the unsettled issues linked and trade-off a move on one for a new condition or a move on something else.
- Be ready to bring back into contention any previously

121

'settled' issues if you need negotiating room under pressure of opposition on a point.

- Memory joggers:
  Remember the big IF
  Never give 'owt' for 'nowt'
  Lead with your conditions
  Keep them linked

8.6 Common avoidable mistakes

- Unconditional proposals
- Asking permission to concede
- Forgetting to state your conditions
- Separating the offer from the conditions
- Separating issues
- Not linking movement on one issue to movement on another
- Using 'If I . . . will you' proposals

9 Closing and Agreeing

9.1 Introduction

The negotiator has two pressures to contend with. The first arises from the basic uncertainty of negotiating: you never really know whether you have squeezed every concession that there is available from your opponent. Hence, you delay making a decision about what is on offer at any moment just in case there is more you can get. The other pressure urges you to settle before your opponent squeezes *you* further. The longer the negotiations continue the more time you have to extract all the concessions available from your opponent but the longer you negotiate the more time he has to do the same to you.

It is not uncommon to find negotiators unable to terminate their negotiations. Unable to close, they keep negotiating, often conceding what appear to be minor concessions which, when added up, can be formidable in cost terms (let alone precedent). These concessions are also avoidable — which is a double penalty. They can be avoided by using closing techniques, some of which will be discussed in this chapter.

If you successfully close a negotiation you must arrive at the eighth and final step, agreement. There is nowhere else to go. An unsuccessful close generally returns you to the argument step and another cycle of bargaining.

This chapter is about closing and agreeing. Practice in closing will enhance your confidence and get you to agreement faster and less expensively than waiting until your opponent decides he has got enough out of you.

9.2 Judging the close

It is not necessary for the parties to be at their respective limits before a negotiation can be concluded. This would imply that their limits coincided on the negotiating continuum. Most often they do not. There is an overlap to a greater or lesser extent. What you are prepared to settle for *in extremis* is generally closer to your opponent's ideal than what he is prepared to settle for. Uncertainty arises because neither side is sure where the other party's limit really is. Hence, you may be prepared to settle at some point which is well inside your limit and which may also be short of his limit. On some other issue he may be pushing the settlement point close to your limit.

There may be greater pressure on you to settle there while you are still in front, near your limit on one issue and nearer your ideal on another. The more issues in dispute the greater the combination of possibilities of distances from your ideals and limits.

This makes the decision to close the bargaining step a matter of judgment. It is, as always, easier to learn *how* to close than *when* to close. Mistiming a close is less serious than not knowing how to close. If it is the wrong time to try to close your opponent will at least let you know about it whereas he is unlikely to help you to close if it is in his interests to keep you bargaining.

If you are on your limit position you will have a strong incentive to try to close. Any further bargaining will draw concessions from you beyond your limits. If your opponent becomes convinced that you really have nothing more to offer he will choose to agree or break off. But it is obvious that you would not be negotiating effectively (or profitably) if you always waited until you were at your limit before you closed, though in closing you might try to create the impression that you were at your limit and that is why you were closing.

Your opponent cannot be sure that when you state 'this is

124

'FINAL' OFFERS

A wage negotiation in a small domestic appliance factory was going badly. The union side were pressing for cash increases for maintenance engineers well beyond the company's budget.

The management negotiator was feeling harassed and the discussions were becoming protracted. In desperation and flustered, the company side quickly put together a revised offer and rushed in to present it to the union. With a flourish it was announced that the union side had to accept the package because it represented the 'final offer *for the moment*'!

Needless to say, more money was needed to settle the deal.

Even the most experienced negotiator can be trapped if he fails to prepare carefully at every stage. It is even more essential to take time in preparing a response when time appears to be running out.

my final offer' it is necessarily true. The fact that you are most likely to close when you are at your limit is not the same thing as saying that when you close you are actually at your limit. You may be closing well short of your limit. It is his job to test your determination to close.

This suggests that the credibility of your close determines how your opponent reacts to it.

Timing your close will be a big factor in its credibility. Again this comes down to judgement. If you try to close too early he will interpret your move, at best, as just another concession in the bargaining step; at worst, as a provocative and hostile act. He may not have finished bargaining when you suddenly try to close. If he feels the exchange of concessions at that point is asymmetrical (he has given away more than you have and he is waiting to move on to other issues to get some concessions from you to balance up the exchange) he will certainly resist leaving off bargaining and entering the close step.

Trying to close too early risks not closing at all. It could prove expensive because, if you have used a 'final offer' close once, it is difficult to use it again with credibility if the negotiations continue and you make concessions beyond your 'final offer'. Deciding what constitutes your final offer is a matter of policy. You will have to make that decision in the light of the progress of the negotiations. In effect, you are deciding whether you prefer not to have a settlement rather than continue to make concessions to reach one later. Bargaining will have produced for both sides an exchange of concessions or the possibility of them. Given the concessions that are on offer ('If you do X, we will do Y') and those already agreed, subject to acceptance of the total package, you must decide whether to end the bargaining and enter the close.

The purpose of closing is to lead you to agreement. That cannot be emphasized too much. It conditions your handling of the close. You are effectively telling your opponent: 'You must now choose to accept things as they stand'. So you must present this in a way that emphasizes both your determination not to concede more and that his best interests lie in settling with you at that point.

Before we go on to look at some of the most common and therefore most successful closing techniques we will outline which features a close should contain. These should help you frame your close.

Closing must, as we have emphasized, be credible. He has to believe you mean what you say. If he tests your credibility you have to be able to reinforce your message, firmly but not provocatively. If he has previous experience of your behaviour during the movement from bargaining to closing this might assist your credibility (though it might not if you fumbled the close last time).

Your closing package must meet enough of his needs to be acceptable. If he prefers continued resistance to accepting certain items, either because he is resolutely opposed to them or because the 'price' is not right, the close will fail: he prefers

AN EXAMPLE OF THE NEED TO CONSTANTLY REMEMBER YOUR OBJECTIVES

A frequent fault in negotiation is when the inexperienced negotiator becomes so entranced by his own arguments and ploys he becomes hooked, like some oratorical junkie, on the debate itself, forgetting that the object is to achieve planned agreements.

In one particularly complex salary negotiation, it had been agreed by the company team, in advance, that they would plan to consolidate some supplementary payments into basic salaries. This would significantly improve the competitive position of their salary bands, involve only a small increase in costs as a result of salary-related items being paid out on a higher basic, and would make the whole deal a more attractive proposition.

The tactical plan was to resist this in the early stages and then use it in the 'close' stage as part of the final package to obtain agreement. The negotiator involved, however, felt that his arguments against consolidation were so convincing that he should abandon the original plan and 'win' this point.

The result was an agreement and therefore a 'win' but salary levels were then totally uncompetitive making recruitment of staff impossible.

Unplanned short-term wins in negotiations are rarely desirable.

'no-deal' to a deal on your closing terms. Consideration of what terms he might settle on must guide your decision on whether a small movement would secure a close as against no movement at all.

The close must be stated in such a way that failure to accept it more or less as it stands will lead your side to prefer no-deal. This arises from the previous two conditions, credibility and acceptability, and also as a cautionary condition for your side. If you do not prefer 'no-deal', because you still have a wide margin, and you are ready to concede in *this* negotiation given the circumstances, and you are, in fact, merely 'trying it on' you must be careful. Your bluff will be called on most occasions and your negotiating position will weaken if it is, if only because, having failed to close once, you will find it extremely difficult to close later. In other words you will be penalized for 'trying it on' by having to make more concessions.

9.3 Concession close

The concession close is the most common close used in negotiating. It terminates the bargaining step by offering a concession to secure agreement. The likely areas where a concession close can be used will have emerged in the packaging and bargaining steps. Possibilities include:

1 Conceding on a major element in your opponent's demands.
2 Conceding on a major stumbling block.
3 Conceding on a minor issue.
4 Introducing a new concession not originally demanded but attractive to your opponent.

You will have to decide on the magnitude of your final concessions. If you make a big concession it may not close the bargaining because your opponent may assume there is yet more to come if he pushes you. If you make a small concession it may be too small to encourage acceptance.

If you can make a concession close using a concession in a minor matter this is preferable to making a concession on a major matter, especially when it involves conceding an important principle. We have already emphasized the importance of not throwing what you regard as minor issues away early on in the negotiation. In the close you may be searching desperately for the kind of minor concessions you threw away earlier on.

However, negotiations can stick on major issues, especially

128

NEW ITEM CONCESSION

A fruit importer telephoned a firm of food brokers and offered to sell a container load of apples. The price he quoted was too high and the broker declined.

The importer, being anxious to sell, was faced with how he could repackage his proposal. He returned with an amended proposal: 'If you will pay me for the consignment within seven days of receiving my invoice I will lower my price to £x a ton'. The broker agreed and the deal was struck at the new lower price.

The broker commented afterwards (to an observer) that both he and the seller knew that payment would not be made on this occasion any faster than normal but honour was satisfied on both sides because the seller was able to reduce his price without collapsing his position.

The buyer had got a better price than he was first offered and the seller had got a price which was still profitable to himself. He had also avoided setting a precedent. Next time he could claim that no discount could be given to the broker because payment did not materialise within seven days of sight of his invoice on the previous occasion.

those involving principles. If you have to consider making some movement in these areas you will want to limit the concession as much as you can. Indeed, if you open the door in these areas at the close of the bargain you may achieve the exact opposite of your intention: instead of closing, the negotiations continue with your opponents in full flight buoyed up by the break-through they believe they have achieved.

To limit a concession in a major area you can present it in a way which precludes further elaboration at the moment, postponing to some future date negotiations on the concession. An example of this could take the following form:

'If you are prepared to accept this package as it stands we will be prepared to accept for a future negotiation the general principle of lay-off payments.'

This kind of closing concession on a major issue was seen in a major national engineering strike. The union struck for a wage increase and an immediate reduction in working hours from 40 to 35 a week. The latter part of the claim was totally resisted by the employers, who were only prepared to move on the money (but still falling short of the union's demand in that area). The final agreement saw very little movement on the money offer the employers had made, coupled with a commitment to reduce working hours by one hour (from 40 to 39) in three years time. The concession was modest in quantity but of immense significance in principle. Having breached the dam the union was quite prepared, in the circumstances of the strike situation, to return to work in response to the concession close.

The concession close is the small step which secures agreement.

If you are absolutely up against the wall and cannot in justice to your interests make a final concession on something that is on the table you can consider making a concession on something that has not been raised in the current negotiations. You could make a concession in some area outside the negotiations. Selecting the appropriate concession requires some imaginative thinking on your part. One way is to reconsider issues which your opponent has raised in the past but which for one reason or another you have resisted. Recalling these issues to your service now may open up the prospect of a concession close which will prove acceptable to your opponent. You must judge the strategic importance of selecting a new concession in this way. If you choose correctly it may lead to a settlement where up to that point you were faced with a deadlock, or a concession in an area which you consider for the moment to be to your disadvantage.

By introducing new items onto the table you could break the deadlock. If it is attractive enough to your opponent he will accept your offer and therefore you must choose the new concession carefully. If the issue has been around for a long time it is more than likely that he will be willing to achieve some movement in a previously closed area. It also has the advantage that it takes the immediate pressure off the still hotly disputed issues. Sometimes the mere fact of movement — any movement — is enough to secure the concession close.

9.4 Summary close

An alternative close, perhaps the second most popular, is the summary close. This terminates the bargaining step by summarizing everything that has been agreed up to then, highlighting the concessions that the opposition have secured from your side, and emphasizing the benefits of agreeing to what is on the table.

You list the extent of the movement each side has made and the mutual gains from agreeing: 'We have come a long way and it would be a great pity after all the sacrifices we have each made, to fail now when agreement can be reached with honour on what is before us'. This kind of statement sometimes precedes and sometimes follows the summary of the potential agreement.

If the other side accepts your summary it will say 'Yes'. It is likely that they will say 'Yes, but' and restate some matter that they regard as still outstanding. This presents you with at least two choices. You can lead into a concession close ('Are you saying that if we move on this outstanding item that you will settle?') or to a formal statement of it being a final offer: 'Gentlemen, we have summarized the agreement as we see it. We cannot emphasize too much to you that we have conceded all we can on these issues. There is no more in the kitty and to prolong negotiations in the hope that there is more would be futile on both our parts. This is our final position and we are asking you now to accept what is on the table — including all the major concessions you have already gained from us — and sign the agreement.' If they accept that it is the end of the road and if they want a deal they will agree. If they do not accept it then it is up to you to demonstrate your commitment to the offer.

9.5 Other common closes

The concession close and the summary close are the two most commonly used closes in negotiating. But there are many others which are sometimes used. There is no particular order or importance in our presentation of them, any more than we insist that the concession and summary close should be used in a particular order. It is perfectly possible to try the concession close before or after a summary close. Indeed, if the concession close has not worked you have not a lot of room other than to make the summary close. If the summary close has not worked you have the option of trying a concession close. The main point to remember is that the concession close is conditional on getting immediate agreement. The summary close can be used less rigidly.

If a summary close has not brought the other side to agreement immediately you can combine it with an *adjournment close*. What you are saying, in effect, is: 'We have summarized the benefits to you of agreeing with what is on offer, we have informed you that this is our final offer and we suggest that we take an adjournment for you to consider what is on offer. We will reconvene the meeting when you are ready to give us your answer.'

It is sometimes necessary to use the adjournment close to allow your opponent time to consider both the offer and the alternatives of not reaching agreement. If an opponent needs such time and you judge it in your interests to allow time you should accommodate him on this point.

The *or else close* is a harder close than the adjournment close. You are presenting him with an ultimatum. Either he accepts what is on offer 'or else'. Presumably the 'or else' has been thought through. If your threat is empty the *or else close* could backfire on you. In its strongest form you are giving him an ultimatum to agree immediately, 'or else'; you can modify this slightly by using the *or else close* with the adjournment close. But adjourning may work to your disadvantage if it gives him time to mobilize a sanction response to deploy against you on re-convening. Moreover, the wider the audience for the *or else close*, the more difficult it is for its receiver to back off without loss of face. If you adjourn, the news has a greater chance of leaking out to your opponent's supporters (in the case of a union). It is a high risk close and you must think very carefully about using it. In most cases we see it used in the heat of the moment by harassed negotiators. In these cases it has the expected effect of raising hostility levels to breaking point. In comparison with the concession close, the *or else close* has a high degree of emotional tension associated with it.

Another close sometimes used by a team operating at their budget limits is the *either/or close*. Here the purpose is to give the opposition the choice of alternatives any one of which is within the budget limits of the closer. It has the advantage that the receiver has some freedom of choice. He divides up what is on offer in the way he considers suits him best. The one thing he cannot do is extend the offer (though it is possible he may ask for a minor adjustment in some item giving you the opening for trying a concession close).

The *either/or close* can be used in company with an *adjournment close*. They can adjourn to consider which of the alternatives they prefer. Its best use is where you have staked out your offer but cannot get it accepted because they want some other distribution, or more likely, more movement on other items as well as the movement you have already made. You are giving them a choice: 'You can have more here and less there, or more there and less here. It's up to you but you cannot have both. We are at our limit and we are prepared to agree to either combination.'

9.6 Agreeing

The purpose of the closing step is to secure agreement to what is on offer. Agreeing is the last step in the negotiation towards which all the others have been working. We negotiate to agree, though in some negotiations we must wonder if the participants appreciate this elementary fact.

WRITTEN RECORDS REDUCE RISKS

A film company approached the author of a successful play, then running in London's West End, and his agent with a view to acquiring the film rights. The parties held a meeting to discuss the proposal and eventually came to an 'understanding'. The author and his agent were willing to sell the film rights if certain difficulties could be overcome respecting some other contractual obligations they were under and if the contract included the points they had raised in the discussions.

At this point each party, in good faith, had a different view as to what had been agreed. This became clear in subsequent weeks when the film producers claimed that the author had agreed to sell the film rights to them and the author claimed that this was 'subject to contract'. As the parties could not agree between them what had taken place the case went to court with the producers suing for breach of oral contract. The author's defence was that no contract had been entered into and would not be because he believed the conditions could not be met.

The result was a long and protracted legal battle plus the attendant personal stress of contesting the action, which threatened to affect the author's creative work. In the end the author won the case with costs.

But all of that could have been avoided if *(a)* each party had been made specifically aware that a negotiation was in process and would not close until a written contract was signed; *(b)* a written summary of the opening discussion had been sent next day to the film producers detailing the conditions that had to be met *before* a contract could be drawn up; *(c)* agreement was reached at every stage on what had been discussed. In nine cases out of ten this may not be necessary but as you do not know if your case will turn out to be the difficult tenth, it is best to cover for the tenth by doing it this way every time.

Agreeing is, however, a very dangerous time for negotiators. There is often a high degree of euphoria present as the tensions of the previous steps dissipate themselves in the natural relief of arriving at agreement. The euphoria can be soporific. It can put you off your guard.

If you are keen to get agreement and relieved that you have achieved it you may not be careful in the finer details of what you have agreed. This can cause endless trouble later on when the agreement is implemented and each side has its own version of what was agreed perhaps some considerable time earlier. Then the charges will fly about: 'cheating', 'mendacity', 'dirty tricks', 'foul play' and so on. The emotional heat caused by feelings such as these can take a long time to overcome. And the worst part of it is that probably there is a genuine error on both sides as to what really was agreed. People can really believe something was agreed when it was not.

The best way to avoid this unpleasantness is to make sure before you leave the table that both sides are absolutely clear on what they have agreed to. Sometimes easier said than done but we suggest you do at least the following.

A detailed summary of each item in the package must be read and agreed between the negotiators. In more formal negotiations there will normally be a working text available. If the negotiations have produced explanatory clauses, or definitions of 'understood meanings', these are usually contained in an appendix to the main agreement but they must be agreed by each side precisely because their purpose is to assist in implementing the agreement. For example, the main text may use a word like 'reasonable' ('the supplier agrees to give reasonable notice of delivery times') and the negotiators may have reached an understanding on what each means by 'reasonable'. If it can be written into an appendix it should be, and if it is to be recorded the form of words to be used must be agreed.

If the negotiations are less formal and the agreement has been summarized orally it may suit you to send a written version of that summary to the other side in the post after the meeting.

135

But the golden rule must be: *summarize what has been agreed and get agreement that what has been summarized was agreed.*

If the other party disagrees with part of your summary, or you with his, then get agreement on that point there and then. The more complex the negotiations the more room there is for confusion and memory lapses (watch out for the 'memory lapse' gambit where your opponent slips in one or two surreptitious concessions on your behalf or pulls back a couple of his own).

If you pay attention you will not be caught out with a dispute of interpretation later on. It is no good being 'too tired' to get the agreement tied down, or 'fed up' with arguing. The negotiator's work is not finished until the agreement step has been completed. Anything less than completion is sloppiness which you will pay for eventually.

9.7   Checklist for closing and agreeing

- Decide where you intend to stop trading.
- Is it credible? Is it too soon for your opponent?
- Which close is more appropriate?
- Has he replied 'yes' to a question from you about whether a concession on your part on some item will cause him to agree to the package? (If he says 'no', you must get all of his objections out before trading any more concessions.) If he has said 'yes' consider the concession close.
- Think whether to lead with the summary close and then try the concession close or *vice versa.*
- What other close could you use?
- If you are going for a 'final offer' are you serious or is it a bluff? Remember, a final offer increases in credibility the more formal it is, the more senior the person delivering it, the more public the audience, the more specific it is and the more specific the time for acceptance. Bluffing 'final offers' can destroy credibility in the current negotiations and in subsequent ones. Do not try to force a 'final offer' under emotional pressure.
- Remember: *adjournment* and *or else closes* have a greater

risk in them than *concession* and *summary closes* (and *either/ or* closes).

- If the close has been successful: what has been agreed?
- List the agreement in detail.
- List the points of explanation, clarification, interpretation and understanding.
- Try to prevent your opponent leaving the table until an agreed summary has been recorded.
- If there is disagreement on an alleged agreement the negotiations must recommence until agreement is reached again.
- If the agreement is oral, send a written note to your opponent of what you believe was agreed as soon as you can after the meeting.

9.8 Common avoidable mistakes

- Inability to terminate bargaining
- Giving away concessions in the closing moments
- Misjudging the timing of a final offer
- Bluffing with a 'final' offer
- Unconditional closing concessions
- Making large concessions at the close
- Not summarizing what has been agreed
- Making inappropriate threats using the *or else close* or the *either/or close*
- Not recording what has been agreed in an acceptable form
- Trying to 'cheat' when recording the alleged agreement

10 Commercial Negotiations

10.1 Introduction

The Eight-step Approach was derived for the most part from the study and analysis of negotiations between management and union representatives in industry and numerous training courses in negotiating skills. Practising negotiators analyzed what went right (and why) and what went wrong (and why) with their own negotiations. It was not long before we began to apply the Eight-step Approach to a wider arena of negotiations, at first informally in discussion of what we read of negotiations published in the media, either at the diplomatic level or the commercial.

It began to dawn upon us that the Eight-step Approach and the associated skills we had identified could be used to analyze most of the negotiations we tried them out on. No matter what standpoint we took: buyer, seller, accountant, diplomat, hijacker, husband, wife or child, the Eight-step Approach was applicable.

The differences between industrial relations and commercial negotiating were certainly apparent, even at the anecdotal level, and any serious consideration of the two environments would confirm, systematically, that these differences were of some significance, if only because they modified the behaviour of participants.

In this chapter we examine some of these differences (and their similarities). We use the eight-step format to illustrate the influences of the commercial environment in which negotiations take place.

10.2 The commercial environment

By commercial negotiations we mean all negotiations conducted in a non labour versus capital environment where monetary values are dominant. This excludes negotiations at the international level between governments on diplomatic or political matters (though it is often the case that commerce is an important part of these types of negotiations, e.g. inter-EEC member negotiations, trade deals and funding of foreign currency transactions) and all negotiations at the domestic level where monetary transactions are excluded.

There are several types of commercial negotiation: bilateral (between buyer and seller), trilateral (more than one competitor) and multilateral (a group negotiation between parties of roughly equal status).

Bilateral negotiations occur when two parties attempt to find acceptable terms of doing business. Neither party is obliged to do business with the other. A management must ultimately settle with its workforce; a consumer does not have to buy a particular producer's product — he can buy another producer's product or something entirely different. In these circumstances there has to be some incentive for both parties to trade. If the available incentives are inadequate they can agree to disagree and part company. The relationship ends.

Continuity of relationship is relative. Relative size is one important factor: IBM and the US Government; Russia and China; two men in a life boat. They may agree to disagree but their behaviour is modified by the knowledge that they may have to agree at some time in the future.

Bilateral 'conflict' negotiations occur where a dispute has arisen as a result of the relationship between the two parties: late delivery, poor performance, component failure and compensation payments for example. The relationship between the parties may be terminated but the conflict remains until settled (in or out of court).

Trilateral 'competitive' negotiations occur where two or

more parties compete with each other to do business with a third. This is extremely common in commercial life but almost unknown in industrial relations. In these circumstances no seller knows what his competitor is doing. He must modify his position in an attempt to anticipate what his competitor is doing. However, as each seller meets the buyer separately they engage in a form of bilateral negotiation.

Multilateral group negotiations occur when a number of parties, all in a permanent relationship with each other, with certain common interests but also definite divergent interests, negotiate on issues that affect all of them. Examples would include the departments of a company or public authority, the members of an international association (EEC) or a military alliance (NATO).

10.3 Commercial practices

If somebody wants something that you have, it has a 'price'. A commercial negotiator's job is to secure that price. Information, goodwill, an order, continuity of supply, an appointment or whatever, everything has its price.

How much will a foreign power pay for secret information? How much is a naval goodwill visit worth? What is the price of a continuous supply of air to a diver? What is a Papal audience worth?

In commercial dealing there is a great tendency on the part of sellers to 'give' without receiving anything in return. If you ask the seller why he did this he will often reply that by doing so he gained 'goodwill'. This may just be a convenient rationalization to justify poor negotiating behaviour: goodwill can be as intangible as a junkie's promise.

All salesmen have a certain 'fear', or reverence, for the buyer. He has the power to give or withhold an order. Too often this leads to an over-apologetic attitude on the part of the seller which weakens his negotiating position. Buyers, informally, revel in retelling stories of how they humbled sellers, but one suspects that the sellers made it easier for them to do so by their attitude. Buyers reinforce the normal 'fear' felt by sellers by their cultivated attitudes of apparent indifference to whether they buy from the particular salesman in front of them or some other. But it is likely that the buyer needs what the salesman is trying to sell as much or more than the seller needs to sell it, more so when the product has unique features that the buyer desires.

Too often salesmen are remote from their company's decision centres. There is a general reluctance on the part of sales managers to delegate negotiating authority to their field sales force because they fear they may give away everything in order to get the order (a fear that is mostly justified by the actions of many salesmen). As a result, the salesman has little room for initiative and must refer to 'head office' even on minor points, thus causing frustration in the buyer (and not a little contempt).

Usually, negotiation takes place at the end of the sale when the buyer is definitely interested but requires additional concessions. The seller having seen the 'rabbit', i.e. the order, is only too willing to overcome the buyer's objections by making additional concessions. The sight of the buyer's pen hovering over the contract induces major concessions as the seller contemplates the prospects of a sale, 'at last'. (Soviet buyers are particularly adept at 'last moment' demands for concessions just before signing the contract.) This always arises because the seller fails to realize he is in a negotiation and not a sales pitch. He has often thrown away most of his concessions in the face of the stony silence of the buyer while he makes his presentation. The buyer might also be unaware he is negotiating. He may have already decided to accept a re-order on the previous terms and is mentally wishing the salesman would 'get on with it'.

Commercial negotiations tend to be conducted on a far more polite level than industrial relations negotiations. Diplomacy, friendliness and co-operation are the norms. There is widespread belief, probably mostly true, that buyers 'buy from those they like' and that sellers give a better deal to 'those they like'. The danger is that this is used as an excuse for achieving a poorer deal than was available.

There is often a reluctance among inexperienced negotiators to divulge information about such sensitive subjects as profit, cash flow, prompt payment and so on. This arises from

141

CASE OF THE CCFs

A major high technology company was in financial trouble, and consultants were called in to help devise a strategy for survival. By accident, one of the consultants was discussing some minor affair with a member of the sales staff and he noticed a large pad of 'no carbon required' forms in the sales person's briefcase.

Asking what they were, he discovered they were 'CCFs', or 'Customer Concession Forms'. Upon inspection these remarkable forms were clearly designed to monitor the scale and frequency of concessions made by the sellers in their daily work to individual clients. The form was most detailed, and required the signed approval of twenty senior managers from various functions before a major concession could be authorized.

The sales person confessed that he used his CCFs regularly (no wonder each seller was issued with a thick pad of them!). 'But what about all these authorization levels you require?' asked the consultant. 'No problem,' replied the seller, 'I just fill in my bit and send them to head office for authorization. Nobody has ever come back to me, or my clients, about anything I have put in.'

Over the next few days, the consultant discovered that almost every seller regularly used the CCFs to go below the company's bottom line price. No sales person had ever been queried about the use of a CCF. The consultant concluded that this was a major source of the company's low profit performance. The remedy was obvious: withdraw the CCFs before the company went bust.

the belief that the other party will use this information to gain an advantage. This may be true in certain circumstances but this kind of information may cause the other party to revise its expectations.

In deciding to divulge information you must certainly consider whether it will expose your weaknesses or whether it will compel your opponent to revise his demands. He has no real interest in 'killing the goose that lays the golden eggs'.

Adjournments are less common in commercial negotiations than they are in industrial relations negotiations in the sense that the adjournments that occur are not as frequent *during* a negotiating session — union negotiators may adjourn several times in a session to consider a management proposal (or lack of one). In commercial negotiations adjournments are more likely to correspond to 'natural breaks' and reconvened sessions a few days hence. This has advantages and disadvantages. It allows additional time for reviews and additional preparation. The drawback is that it may allow the competition to get in, either in the form of another buyer, or another seller.

It may, therefore, be useful for commercial negotiators to cultivate the notion of short adjournments to 'give serious consideration to the new proposals or new information' presented during the session.

The co-operative atmosphere of a commercial negotiation allows for a greater range of signals. The same rule applies: *listen*.

Many commercial negotiations do not take place face to face. This is less satisfactory for exercising negotiating skills. The telephone limits the readability of signals and imposes an awkward time constraint. The letter leads to entrenchment of positions and inhibits flexibility. Negotiating via a third party leads to misinterpretations caused by the problems of briefing the third party adequately to handle all the expected nuances of the opponent's position. Meeting the other party face-on is by far a better negotiating stance: misunderstandings can be corrected in seconds and adjustments can be made to meet contingencies as they arise.

Intermediaries, like Dr Henry Kissinger at the international level, are used less in commerce though most Arab

'COLD WAR'

A major Scottish civil engineering machinery manufacturer with a world-wide reputation secured a contract to supply its equipment to an Eastern European country. When delivery was made the government purchasing agency rejected the equipment as being 'technically sub-standard'. This was widely reported in the trade press.

The real, but undisclosed, reason for non-payment was a shortage of hard currency in the client country.

The manufacturer protested and demanded a retraction of what it regarded as totally unwarranted criticism of its products. This met with no response. For the agency to admit the real reason for not being willing to pay for the machinery would engage it in embarrassing domestic complications.

The chairman of the company made a policy decision not to sell any more equipment to this country until he received a retraction because without the retraction his company's reputation would be compromised.

Eventually, a 'form of words' acceptable to both sides, was agreed and their relationship has resumed.

countries at present insist on using their own nationals as intermediaries keeping the foreign dealers at arm's length. This proved to be a most profitable role for many Middle East 'middle men' who are able to 'cream it off' at both ends of the transaction.

The final important difference in the commercial world is the law of contract. It is generally enforceable in the courts. The position is more complicated in international commercial negotiations because of differences in laws and assumed liabilities. But, nevertheless, the courts are a source for remedies if contracts are broken. Suing defaulting contractors is a far more likely event than suing a defaulting union. A sound knowledge of contract law is therefore essential for negotiators drawing up an agreement (remembering that in Scotland a verbal offer once accepted is a binding contract whereas, for example, in Russia and Eastern Europe contracts are only binding if, and for as long as, the government agrees that they are).

10.4 Preparation for the commercial environment

Preparation by commercial negotiators is of no less import-ance than with other negotiators. Fortunately many companies invest resources in preparation as part of their everyday activities. What is the marketing function if not applied preparation? Knowing one's own product and the customer's needs it is designed to serve is an elementary aspect of preparation for a commercial negotiator. The more complex the product the more intensive the preparation, the wider the market and the greater the information flow that has to be digested.

A commercial negotiator for a large computer company explained his success (which included a level of earnings in one year greater than his company chairman's) by intensive preparation, every evening and at weekends, even getting his wife to test run him through his product specifications and client requirements. He worked at it until he knew it all backwards and then went in and negotiated with his potential client. Such was his grasp of detail about both his product's capabilities and his client's needs that his negotiating opponent was compelled to rely upon his judgement about many issues. This must have enabled him to pitch his pack-ages right where they could do him nothing but good.

Of course, that level of motivated preparation is unusual but it certainly shows that it pays off. Studying market survey reports is one way of getting to know what you are up against. They also provide you with information about where you should direct your efforts. And they test the realism of your negotiating objectives by indicating trends and possible market shares.

Knowing what is happening in the market is one half of preparation: knowing what your company can realistically do in the market is the other. Matching your own product's performance against customer needs is an essential part of developing a negotiating strategy: if he is to be convinced that your product matches his needs you must first convince yourself.

There is a vast amount of information about any market available at little cost of time, effort and money. Most of this can cross your desk on a daily basis. Among these items we suggest the following:

Daily newspapers (in Europe the *Financial Times* for example).

Trade papers.

Professional journals.

Government publications, both domestic and export topics.

Reports prepared by most major banks, e.g. Barclays Bank Intelligence Unit Reports: available for every country and for many products, free.

Private reports sold on a commercial basis (Economist Intelligence Unit for example).

Reports by stockbrokers and merchant banks.

Company analysis services (in the UK, for example, EXTEL).

Trade and commercial association reports.

Consular services both at home and abroad.

Trade missions.

International commodity agencies reports.

The 'grapevine', i.e. meet your colleagues and competitors informally.

If you are going to be negotiating with foreign nationals it would obviously pay you to consult your library on the history of their country and on its current political-cum-economic arrangements. (Not, we hasten to add, in order to engage them in discussion of their political views but to give yourself background in the influences that probably determine their outlook.)

146

10.5 Commercial argument

The argument step in commercial negotiations tends to be more polite than it is in industrial or international negotiation, at least where it involves one side making a presentation of its offer to a potential buyer. But remember, commercial partners often fall out over all kinds of issues and the client may enter the negotiation with a strongly held view that the other party has 'sold them short' or failed in some way to meet a contractual obligation. Thus, the negotiations may not get heated but they certainly can be very 'cold'.

There is no doubt that moving the discussions from the grievance to the proposed, or possible, remedies is one very effective way of handling the hostility of this opening step. Making up for lost time from a late delivery, or lost output from a failure of performance, usually involves somebody paying compensation in some form or another. This is a negotiable issue. Limiting the financial damage to your company is an obvious objective and the L-I-M format will help in sorting out what priority you give to various combinations of financial packages you can devise.

Listening for signals is absolutely critical. Moving from 'never darken our doorstep again' to 'let's put this experience behind us and look to the future' may actually be only a small step. But you must listen for the shift in their use of language from the absolute to the non-absolute: 'we will never buy from you again' to 'what guarantees have we that this disaster will not happen again?'

10.6 Commercial bargaining

Commercial negotiations may commence with an exploratory session during which the client is specifying his needs and expecting you to come back, then or later, with a proposal of how your company will meet those needs. Drafting that proposal may involve considerable expense (think of a major building contract, or a consultant's report on a management problem). The meeting to discuss your proposal is part of the negotiation. Normally, he will expect you to have padded

147

your proposal with a negotiating margin. This introduces once again all we have said about handling concessions with extreme care and structuring the negotiations so that concessions are exchanged. If you cannot change the price, change the package: 'Our price is for that package, if you want a different package we have a different price, or if you want a different price we have a different package'. You must imaginatively introduce variables into your package which enable you to keep your broad proposal to deal with his problems on the table. This is where your preparation pays off, or does not if you have not done it properly. The most difficult thing you have to contend with is when you are required to put in a 'one offer only' tender. In which case you will have to commence your negotiations right at the specification session, carefully identifying your opponent's priorities and attempting to structure the specification towards the simplest package you can devise, which should be, by definition, the one with the lowest price.

One way to do this is to divide the proposal into its elements: so much for the basic product and staged amounts for 'extras'. The client can buy the entire package or the parts he wants or can afford. He chooses the level of service your product can provide for his interests. For instance, in packaging a training course it might be necessary to propose a basic fee for the tuition, a 'hotel' charge for the course, depending on venue, a hire charge for the video equipment and technician, plus the course expenses. The 'one offer only' tender, then, has several variables in it which, though the proposer is not present to negotiate, the receiver is compelled to 'negotiate' with himself by selecting which price level he wants to reach.

It is common in commercial dealings to have various levels of price to suit the extent of the service required by the client: an 'ex-works' price, a price at the client's factory gate, an installation price and an in-service price. Payments may be agreed on despatch, on receipt, or in-working-order. The opportunities for packaging are immense, for example, on credit terms. The general rule of making all concessions conditional applies with the same force in commercial negotiations as elsewhere: 'If you are prepared to adjust your payment terms we are prepared to alter our deliveries'. The benefits of keeping issues linked are apparent even at a casual glance. Obstacles to an agreement are best handled by linking them to concessions on other issues. ('If you wish to speed delivery it is possible for you to collect the batches as they come off our lines instead of waiting for our own transport to deliver to you.')

The scope for packaging and bargaining is almost endless provided the negotiators are fully conscious of what variables are present or what can be created. If they always seek out variables to trade-off they will get better deals than otherwise. Nothing for nothing is not an insult to your opponent. He is in business because he is used to handling valuable properties. The monetary basis of commerce lends itself to imaginative marginal adjustments. Dealing is the ethos of the activity. Therefore, use it to your advantage.

Closing is no different in commercial bargaining from any other negotiation. The final concession to secure the deal is well known: car salesmen use it all the time: 'Tell you what I'll do, Mr Customer, buy the car at £5,000 against a trade-in price on your old car of £2,000 and I'll tax and insure the car for a year. OK?')

People often use the adjournment close as a polite way of breaking off from the negotiation: 'I will have to think about it' or 'I will have to consult my boss/wife', etc. The *or else* close is seldom used except in a threat of legal action. It is, however, implicit in the commercial relationship that agreement is reached *or else* you will do business elsewhere. This does not create a blackmail situation because it is normally also implicit that the other party is prepared to take the alternative rather than do business on non-viable terms.

11 Industrial Relations

11.1 Introduction

The differences between commercial and industrial relations negotiations are illuminating. In the commercial environment the seller operates in some trepidation of the buyer because the buyer can go elsewhere to get what he needs. The buyer of labour operates against a different background. He may have very sound reasons for being in trepidation of the seller.

The circumstances in which a seller can put a buyer out of business are very rare. But many companies have gone out of business or have been commercially crippled because the labour force has immense power. It is inevitably so. It is undesirable for many reasons that it should be any different. Because if it were different, labour would require to be a directed body of wage-slaves with no freedom to sell their labour collectively at the highest rate they can get. This refers, of course, only to those societies where labour is free. In Russia the 'liberation of the proletariat' has precluded free negotiations of labour prices. Negotiations take place on fulfilling the production plan.

In free societies the buyer/seller relationship in industrial relations serves to illustrate the need for structured negotiated agreements.

Unions and management often perceive their relationship as being dominated by their conflict of interests. These are often formulated as 'zero sum', or negatively related interests: when unions make gains, management correspondingly loses.

150

Consider the following objectives that might be relevant for each side, and note how a positive gain (+) for one of the parties is seen as a negative pay-off (−) for the other:

Objective	Union's pay-off	Management's pay-off
Strengthening the union	+	−
Welfare of union members	+	−
Union control over work	+	−
Political goals of the union	+	−
Ambitions of union officials	+	−
Strengthening the company	−	+
Management control of work	−	+
Commercial criteria for decisions	−	+
Goals of the company	−	+
Ambitions of management personnel	−	+

Developing policies to achieve any of these objectives is bound to become an issue between union and management. Attempts to raise welfare spending on union members may be resisted by a management trying to divert resources into acquisitions to strengthen the company's growth prospects. Similarly, an ambitious manager trying to keep an operation within budget may be resisted by a union anxious to maintain its control over the way work is carried out by management.

The conflict need not be impossible to resolve. Head-on challenges to important objectives can lead to difficult situations. A union that directly attacks an important managerial perogative (the hiring and promotion of employees) can expect fierce resistance from management. But within each broad objective, there is room for negotiation to search for a compromise. There is also room for trading across objectives. The union could accept movement on managerial control of work in exchange for 'no redundancy' agreements, or the right to be consulted about any proposed changes.

11.2 External influences

In industrial relations there are external influences on both parties of a social, political and economic kind. Employers have to contend with government legislation, particularly in national prices and incomes policies and 'unfair dismissal' law. They must also consider the policies of their national employers' associations. In the past, members of the Engineering Employers Federation were expelled for breaking ranks in a pay dispute by conceding to the unions' demands in the midst of a national strike. It is inconceivable that a company would be expelled from the Employers' Federation for buying 'widgets' at a higher price than the other members but they were expelled for buying labour above the Federation 'price'.

Unions are bound by the policies of their annual conferences and the policies of the TUC, or AFL-CIO, or their equivalents in other countries. They are strongly influenced by the politics of the political parties they are affiliated to or are sympathetic towards. All these influences can be brought to the negotiating table on issues which are ostensibly quite separate. The public face of the main negotiators is, therefore, quite different from their private face.

LATE BARGAINING COUNTER

The late introduction of a new element into a negotiation has dangers attached to it, but it can be very productive if handled carefully.

'Our engineers have been examining your proposals in great detail and we feel that if you were to offer an automatic feed device it would certainly meet our requirements.'

'This model cannot accommodate an auto-feed.'

'That is unfortunate. In that case we should require a more attractive price package to make this acceptable.'

Recently, a major union in Britain negotiated a private medical deal for its members who were working on 'away from home' contracting. This would be common in the US but totally out of line in Britain with its National Health Service (which incidentally did not adequately cover these workers while away from home). Their agreement was condemned by the TUC and the Labour Party, which placed constraints upon other unions and employers who were willing and able to agree to similar deals. The result has been that employers have sometimes introduced 'private' health schemes for employees either on a voluntary basis or separately from negotiations from unions. Despite union opposition, such schemes are increasingly common and popular with union members.

External influences constrain negotiating freedom but in the homogeneous society existing in Britain this has to be faced as a fact of life.

11.3 Negotiations in the industrial environment

The management negotiator will know from Chapter 3 the vital need to prepare effectively. He must establish his L-I-M objectives and estimate his opponent's interests and perceptions of the issues. Like the salesman who researches his target market, the manager must develop his methods of assessing his opponent's objectives and priorities. The most common means are:

1   Informal discussion with union officials and shop steward representatives.
2   Regular reading and research of trade union journals, the 'Left Wing' press and TUC documents. (This should include the 'underground' press circulating among the workforce.)
3   Frequent contact between managers, supervisors and the shop or office floor.

One major multinational company relies on anonymous opinion polls and attitude surveys conducted among its employees. Good prior intelligence will minimize, although not eliminate, unnecessary arguments in the opening step of the negotiation, leaving the negotiator prepared to confirm or modify his prepared assumptions.

The argument step in industrial relations is particularly delicate and especially prone to personal hostility. Ideological barriers exist and normal workplace antagonisms can dominate. The language tends to be more colourful than that employed by salesmen with their buyers.

It is important that the negotiator at least understands the continuing relationship between the sides of industry and makes the most productive use of the argument step.

The point-scoring technique is least helpful and at its most dangerous in industrial relations.

Management negotiators, when faced with the abusive harassing tactics of an opponent (the 'erupting volcano'), are advised to adopt a 'low profile'. Listening intently to what is being said, questioning and absorbing the onslaught, is the best way to pick up the inevitable signals given out in an uncontrolled emotional spasm. Eventually, the 'volcano' will exhaust his emotional reserve of insults and the negotiations can move forward, using the information gained and the signals displayed in uncontrolled argument.

It is relatively easy to develop the skill of non-response to these kinds of outbursts, even if you have an impatient and intolerant nature, especially when you realize the tangible benefits to be gained from doing so and the short-lived nature of this type of hostility.

It is not uncommon for management and union representatives who have been at desperate loggerheads in a negotiation to be found subsequently in convivial personal conversation a short time later. It is therefore particularly important for the negotiator to be able to separate the bargaining role from his personal relationships.

However, keeping personal feelings out of the negotiating relationship is dependent upon the hostility remaining private to the participants. That is why the most fatal error in industrial relations is for anybody involved to 'go public' in the argument phase. Even where the negotiations appear to be intractably broken down it is vital to persist and attempt to move the argument into the signalling, packaging and bargaining steps.

DON'T TAKE IT PERSONALLY

One senior manager in a textile company in the East Midlands of England was seen, to the astonishment of some of his colleagues, playing the piano for a trade union pensioners' party the very night after the trade union officials had formally complained in writing to the managing director that he was, what they called, a 'retrograde' influence and 'personally responsible for every problem they had', past, present and future. The official who signed the letter of complaint was the one who asked the manager to help out at the union social.

DON'T GO PUBLIC

One company, in the south of England, could not reach a settlement on a wage deal and was experiencing strike action. The management were convinced that the workforce, if given a free choice, would see things their way and repudiate their union officials and the local union stewards. They bought advertising space in the local evening newspaper and attacked the union officials, revealed the contents of their private discussions with the officials, and crowned it all by describing the 70 per cent of their total workforce who were on strike as an 'irresponsible minority'. The criticisms the management had made may or may not have been valid. The point is that 'going' public in the argument phase prejudices relationships for a long while to come.

The opposite kind of personality to cope with beside the 'erupting volcano' is the 'strong, silent type'. He simply states his demand and refuses to budge on anything. Again infinite patience is required. He must be subjected to polite and

155

firm questioning, always seeking reasons for his position and therefore signals about his objectives. He must be encouraged to propose the remedy as well as the grievance. It is essential to continue seeking for information and for his signals rather than reacting similarly with stubbornness and non-communication.

While the argument and signalling steps in an industrial relations negotiation may be frequently more emotional, colourful and unguarded than in the commercial situation, the proposal step may be formal and ritualized. The most obvious example is the written claim, submission or demand: in other words, a set of proposals which actually precede the negotiating meeting. Claims must neither be discarded as irrelevant or excessive, nor must they be taken over-seriously. The press are frequently guilty of the latter. Headlines scream 'Miners claim 65% pay increase' and the experts immediately predict appropriate dire consequences for the economy. It must always be remembered that a claim is a claim and a settlement is a settlement. A claim is a proposal of one side's ideal. Unless it is the rare claim which overlaps the limit of the other side, it will not represent the settlement of the negotiation. It may, however, contain signals of concessions even at this stage. For this reason, while it should be treated as the statement of the union's ideal, it must be examined carefully to permit counter-proposals to be formulated and packaged. Written counter-proposals or management 'claims' are rare in the UK but appear much more frequently in the rest of Europe, particularly in Scandinavia, and the United States.

In any event, formal proposing and counter-proposing, written or verbal, are to be encouraged in industrial relations negotiations. As we have seen, the argument step is more emotional and therefore potentially more dangerous to your interests.

The formality and ritual of proposals and counter-proposals are to be encouraged since they help defuse the emotion and move the negotiation more speedily to the productive step of bargaining. Opponents in an industrial relations negotiation can be covertly coached in this technique by the frequent use of adjournments. Thus, a claim or a proposal should, after clarification only, be followed by an adjournment to seriously consider what has been proposed. This adjournment should be followed by a counter-proposal. Suggestions should accompany the counter-proposal that it would best be considered in a further adjournment. The formality of proposing, adjourning and counter-proposing discourages reversion to the argument step and creates the right bargaining atmosphere.

11.4 Unique aspects of union negotiations

The manager negotiating with trade unions has to bear in mind some unique aspects of his environment. Among these we can include the 'folk memory' of the trade union movement. Their attitudes are influenced by the folk myths handed down through the collective memory of their movement. Even the fresh and newly appointed official or shop steward will, by some idealogical osmosis, absorb these folk myths and condition himself to react in certain ways. Much of this collective memory is a genuine expression of the social history of the country, but much of it is also historical illusion. Any suggestion, for instance, of the mildest government legislation in the field of industrial relations is by definition 'a fundamental attack on basic trade union rights'. Memories of the Tolpuddle Martyrs, the General Strike, the 1983 Industrial Relations Act, the 1985 Coal strike, and the 1986 printers lock-out at Wapping, will be brought into the speeches. Suggestions about overmanning or productivity provoke memories of the Great Depression, mass unemployment and poverty.

The negotiator must learn to package proposals in such a way that the folk memories are not prodded by unwise and careless drafting.

The greatest offence, however, is to question the legitimacy of the representatives of a union, its officers or its stewards. This cuts to the very heart of a trade union's reason for existing and it is a very confident, or very foolish, manager who calls its legitimacy into question.

Michael Edwardes, then Chairman of British Leyland,

challenged the unions in 1979 on the representative nature of their views on the future of the company. He called a ballot of the employees and got a resounding 7:1 vote in favour of the plans put forward by his Board of Directors and rejected by the unions. He won in unique circumstances. If he had lost what would his job have been worth?

There is no doubt, however, that the failure of the National Union of Mineworkers to ballot for a national strike in 1985 was an indication of how unrepresentative the union leaders were on this issue. The employers hammered at this weakness throughout the strike and in the end the 'return-to-work' of disgruntled miners brought the strike to an end. Many miners did not strike from the start, and they quoted the lack of a ballot as their reason for repudiating their leaders.

The normal reaction is for the membership to close ranks in solidarity with their leaders under the collective memory that 'unity is strength'. Wise negotiators leave this minefield to the reckless.

Industrial relations negotiations do have some additional unique features which can be best summarized as 'double standards'. New negotiators will quickly learn the way the game is played. Some of the more obvious verbal 'games' are the following:

1   Union policy is normally to demand shorter working weeks but 'management has created a major problem for our members by cutting the overtime they can work'.
2   Equal pay is absolutely correct as long as the men always get more money than the women.
3   You must improve the wages of the lower paid and you must also restore the differential after you have done so.
4   If management cannot make an agreement here and now with us, we prefer to deal with the organ grinder rather than the monkey. However, 'we will now report back to our members to see whether they accept what you have proposed'.
5   The effect of legislation intervening in free collective bargaining is a basic assault on trade union rights. 'We demand legislation on industrial democracy, trade union immunities, industrial planning agreements, compulsory time off' and so on.

6   'Our ban on overtime, together with the work to rule and
     go-slow, is a moderate protest reaction to management's
     unreasonable stance. Your action in suspending our
     members is an outrageous provocation and can only
     serve to worsen the prospects of a settlement'.

There are, of course, numerous managerial double standards
too, but we will leave them to readers to compose from their
own experiences!

The major difference between agreeing and closing in
industrial relations and commercial negotiations is the
requirement of the union side to seek confirmation by the
membership. This means that frequently the final agreement
is not signed, sealed and delivered at the negotiating table.
The objective in these circumstances is to secure the
maximum possible commitment of the trade union side to the
recommended settlement. This means you should ensure that
the closing agreement includes a commitment from them to
recommend acceptance to the workforce. This must be
coupled with the strongest possible message of finality. This
strengthens you, the agreement and the union's recommen-
dation when it is put to the workforce.

12 International Relations

12.1 Introduction

Nations can be in deep conflict. They can threaten or use violence against each other in pursuit or defence of their interests. They can also be in total accord, and the use of threats or sanctions of any kind in pursuit of their interests would be alien to them.

12.2 Recognition

The common feature of relations between sovereign powers is the fact of, and mutual recognition of, each other's sovereignty. To overtly, or covertly, challenge the other party's sovereignty would be regarded as a hostile act. Mutual respect of each other's sovereignty is an essential pre-condition for them having relations. This echoes the sensitivity of trade union officials to their standing as the legitimate voice of the union membership. The analogy can be pushed a little further: countries exist in the international community if they are recognized as countries complete with functioning states. Recognition is a highly valued prize, hence the importance countries place on achieving recognition from the international community – the litmus test of national legitimacy. Unions also strive hard for recognition and do not easily give it up once they achieve it. Unions also compete with each other for recognition. So do competing states for the same territory. Inter-union disputes for recognition are as intractable sometimes as inter-state disputes for recognition (China and Taiwan 'China', Israel and Palestine, Britain and Argentina, Greece and Turkey, are major examples).

While governments have working rules for awarding recognition to other governments they occasionally find an interest in using or withholding recognition as a bargaining counter. The refusal of existing states to recognize the UDI of the Turkish part of Cyprus in 1984 was instrumental in re-opening negotiations between the Turkish and Greek communities. Unless a state is 'recognized', for all intents and purposes it does not 'exist'. Hence, some states receive recognition from one bloc but not from another. For example, the Soviet bloc recognized the Vietnam backed Kampuchea government when it was installed in power by force. Many non-soviet states have refused recognition for years, even though the contenders for recognition are two varieties of communists.

Parties claiming sovereignty actively seek recognition and are hostile or friendly to existing states dependent on their attitude to their claims. This has significance if the regimes in power change. If the incoming regime has grievances about its earlier non-recognition there can be repercussions in subsequent relationships. A classic example would be General de Gaulle's subsequent hostility to Britain and America during his second administration because of his perceptions of how they treated his government-in-exile during the Second World War.

Thus, sovereignty can be a very sensitive pre-condition for longer-term negotiating behaviour. Public and private behaviour at the level of contact between nominally equal parties in respect of sovereignty has some of the aspects of commercial negotiation: polite, respectful and low key. Diplomats are not expected to act other than diplomatically, no matter what the provocation. Commercial negotiators are not expected to insult prospective customers.

12.3 Negotiating fora

The important international conventions for negotiations between sovereign powers are not strictly codified, though some are in the United Nations Charter. Nations are not supposed to militarily attack each other for instance. They do however. War is a common feature of the present international scene. But like all informal (and formal) conventions of behaviour they are only valuable if the parties to them abide by them. Aggressive actions by a sovereign power against another are generally condemned, but without a supranational body to enforce such conventions the condemnation is likely to be moral rather than physical.

World public opinion is a factor in international negotiations. The propaganda war for wide support of a particular way of life is very real. Public opinion works most effectively in countries with political systems that permit public expression of the public's rather than just the government's views. Negotiators from democratic countries have to contend with the effect of public opinion to a much greater extent than negotiators from countries with dictatorship and censorship.

Some countries have entered into voluntary arrangements to have their disputes decided by international law agencies, such as the EEC member's right of reference to a supranational court. This does not necessarily remove the causes of conflict but it certainly influences the negotiating relationships. The more important the influence of legal remedy in a future dispute over what has been agreed, the greater the drafting problems of the agreements being negotiated. Binding treaties involve complex negotiations. The number of possible issues that can be raised increases with the complexity of the many considerations that have to be balanced in finding a form of words satisfactory to the parties' interests.

One result of this situation is to make it common practice to conduct major international negotiations with a plenary committee making the major decisions on principles and to have several smaller sub-committees, or working parties, tackling the details. As the details are agreed by the sub-committees they are referred back to the plenary sessions for final decision and agreement. If the sub-committees cannot reach a decision on something it is clearly an unexpected major issue or has implications for a major issue and this can be redefined for the plenary agenda. This practice is necessary if only to save time. It requires considerable co-ordination of the negotiating team by the team leaders and a great deal of team discipline.

12.4 Preparing for international negotiation

We can apply the Eight-step Approach to international negotiation. This presentation must necessarily be brief but it will serve to underline the points we have been stressing in earlier chapters.

Governments employ specialists in foreign affairs to study and to update their data on countries the government may deal with or on particular topics it may negotiate multilaterally. Hence, the Foreign Office employs literally thousands of man-hours every day in this detailed preparation just in case it is needed by the government. Ministers must try to digest hundreds of briefs and position papers written for them on whatever they are dealing with at a particular time. The more important the negotiation the more thorough the preparation.

People become political leaders precisely because they have some flair, in the main, for working under this kind of pressure. They also have some considerable knowledge of world politics and their country's interests before they assume office, if only because they have to serve a long 'apprenticeship' working their way to the top job. There are, of course, exceptions. But even the most well prepared person has to make additional efforts in preparation on specific issues.

In the Strategic Arms Reduction Talks (START) professional diplomats do most of the detailed negotiating on a face-to-face basis. They take their instructions from their respective governments. When the time comes for the final negotiations and the signing of a Treaty, the preparation involved is considerable. The US President will receive briefing papers from his National Security Council, the State

Department and the Departments of the Treasury, Agriculture, Energy and Commerce. He will receive CIA assessments on what the Soviets are up to around the world, including reports on their covert activities, the objectives of their military deployments, and full details of the political biographies of the highly secretive Soviet leadership. Additional background information would include videotapes of Soviet leaders meeting with Western leaders.

Preparation is then an all day, every day task for international negotiation. Its importance can never be stressed too often.

12.5 On going public

The argument step at this level of negotiation can be anything from stormy to soporific. When great issues are at stake there is bound to be tension. Nations can have collective grievances which are felt with all the emotional pain of an individual, except it is multiplied several times over. Similar rules apply to arguments at the international negotiating table as to those closer to home. There are also a couple of useful points to reinforce what has been said.

The greatest pressure on political leaders is their national image. In the democracies this is both an advantage and a disadvantage: it keeps the people informed of what is being done in their name but it tempts the politician (perhaps to avoid the opposition party making mischief) to 'go public'.

'Going public' is a risky business. Some leaders make their negotiating objective public before they meet the other party. This makes life very difficult, particularly as the public objective is of necessity an ambitious one (it's no good announcing that you are going to seek a modest goal if you are image-building your own importance). If the leader does not achieve the public goal he has 'failed'; if he achieves a more modest goal than his public one he has also 'failed'. But given that it takes two to agree, the public goal may have been totally unrealistic.

The habit of going public by political leaders is understandable but also impolitic. If you 'win' your opponent 'loses' and he too has a public (in communist countries the 'public' is the state apparatus, including the leader's rivals). The more specific your public stance and the more extreme your demands the more difficult it is to get a settlement.

Probably even worse than going public with your objectives before the negotiation is the habit of going public on the arguments themselves. The same pressures to do so are present as with the objectives. It can have even more disastrous results. If you give your version of the arguments between yourself and the other leader, he, or she, must reply in kind. Instead of an argument in private you get an argument in public. Leaders trying to manipulate public opinion in this way make life more difficult for their overall objectives of getting a settlement.

The negotiations between President Sadat of Egypt and Premier Begin of Israel were conducted in absolute secrecy at Camp David in America. The result was remarkable given the state of enmity between the two countries. There would in all probability have been no successful outcome if each side had felt it. necessary to make public statements. As it was, neither leader met in the negotiation until the very end. The Americans shuttled back and forth between the guest houses Begin and Sadat stayed at during the Camp David 'talks'. Without President Carter's personal intervention, and willingness to keep the leaders negotiating, if only by proxy, even the privacy of Camp David would have been insufficient to get agreement. In contrast, negotiations over Britain's net contributions to the EEC have always been an intensely public affair, beginning with Prime Minister Thatcher's public airing of the arguments between her and other leaders at the 1979 Dublin Summit and continuing at later summit meetings. The urge to go public, combined with the very genuine interest of the media in the contents and tone of the negotiations, make it very difficult for leaders to modify their original stances without appearing weak. More recent EEC summits have been less public, and, not surprisingly, greater progress has been made. It is easier, of course, to get agreement in private when the interests of the parties are not in deep conflict. It is the conflict that promotes 'publicness' in the first place, and going public makes the conflict worse.

The great problem in conducting negotiations between countries is the distance that separates them. Either the parties travel to meet each other or permanent teams are located close together. The first makes signalling difficult due to the shortage of time together (leaders have countries to run) and the second makes progress difficult due to the lack of seniority of the negotiators.

CONFUSING SIGNALS

The 1969–73 negotiations between the United States and North Vietnam on the ending of the Vietnam war illustrate the costs of this situation. The teams met rarely, causing problems in their mutual signalling. This was compounded by 'meeting' at four, if not five, levels: both sides 'met' in public exchanges of view at governmental levels, such as President Nixon's addresses to his own public opinion or Hanoi's public statements in world forums; the permanent negotiating teams met in Paris, led by William Porter for the Americans and Madame Nguyen Thi Bhin for the Vietcong, and, at secret meetings, Henry Kissinger met Le Duc Tho, for non-public sessions. American contacts with Hanoi through the Russian Government constituted a fourth level. The war was contact at a fifth level.

The signals emanating from these different levels were not always clear to each side nor mutually consistent. Sometimes the Vietcong delegation would appear to be saying something different from Hanoi, sometimes America appeared to say something different, depending on who was talking.

12.6 Formal proposals

International negotiations tend to be much more formal than their industrial or commercial counterparts. Even if the leaders work on a personal level and without common documentation on the broad issues, their subordinates will use common documentation on almost all occasions. This is essential when working in more than one language. Skills in drafting forms of words are in great demand. So is patience and stamina. Deadline negotiating is sometimes used which forces the parties to come to a settlement by a specific date or even specific time. These sessions provide studies in 'brinkmanship'. In the EEC, deadline negotiating is often combined with non-stop negotiating, with the parties remaining in session without a break until they get an agreed settlement. The combination of the stress of brinkmanship and exhaustion tends to produce the 'historic' compromises for which the EEC has become famous. This has induced the tactic of avoiding deadlines — which avoids making a decision — by those parties who prefer the *status quo*.

Another tactic to facilitate agreement when a deadline is reached is to 'stop the clock'. All parties present agree that the conference clock be stopped at two minutes before the deadline. The fiction is accepted, and the negotiations continue for as many hours or days as is necessary to reach agreement. The minutes show that the negotiation was completed within the deadline, and with agreement the clock is started again.

12.7 Linking proposals

The most important decision on an international issue is whether to link up issues in dispute. The French tried on several occasions to link up Britain's share of the EEC budget with other issues, such as fishing and meat imports policy but was rebuffed by Britain; in 1984 Britain, to the consternation of France, insisted on linking her budget demands to any vote to increase the almost exhausted Common Agricultural Policy budget. The Americans have long had a policy of attempting to link human rights issues to negotiations on disarmament and trade with Soviet bloc countries (most noticeably in 1983 with Poland) but this has not generally been successful. Countries resist giving in to this kind of pressure because it sets dangerous precedents for continued interference in their affairs.

If a country demands that issues be linked it is because the linking helps them. But as the other country perceives that the linking of these issues is to its disadvantage, it resists linking. This reduces to a problem of which side needs the agreement most? In international negotiations this can lead to a deadlock, which each side loses from, but neither can make the necessary moves to re-open a search for settlement. The problem festers, as many international disputes confirm, for years or decades. For example, the British–Albanian dispute over compensation for sinking a ship at the end of World War II, or the Soviet–Japanese 40 year old dispute over islands annexed in 1945.

During complex negotiations the internal issues may be linked even if external issues are kept separate. The then Russian Foreign Minister, Andrei Gromyko, in a difficult moment in the SALT negotiations, put it well: 'If you were to isolate one of these questions and take it out of the general context, it might lend itself to a fairly easy solution. Only you cannot isolate these questions. . . . If I had a ball of twine at my disposal I could show you that graphically.'

12.8   Coercion

Nations in dispute are subject to two sets of pressures: those that lead to attempts to coerce each other, and those that lead them to try compromise.

The ultimate form of coercion is war, but this has substantial costs and, especially in the nuclear age, substantial risks. These costs and risks, including the risk of losing, constrain countries from engaging in coercion to the extent that war breaks out. In other words, the preferred form of coercion is the threat rather than its implementation.

Compromise is both attractive in that it produces a solution without coercion and its associated risks, but it is also constrained by the desire to avoid total surrender, which has its own costs.

This tension between the benefits of coercion, short of war, and the benefits of compromise, short of surrender, guides the foreign policy of most states in conflict. The domestic debate inside the power elite, divides crudely into the factions of 'hawks' and 'doves'; those that prefer a coercive solution and those that prefer compromise. Each attributes to the other faction disreputable interpretations of their behaviour and intentions (the 'hawks' are accused of recklessness with the lives of citizens; the 'doves' are accused of 'betraying' the interests of fellow citizens).

Threats are the instrument of coercion. A country threatens another in one of two ways: either it threatens to cause harm to it, or its interests, if the country does not do something, or it threatens harm if it does something. The former threat is one of compliance: 'do what I say, or else'. The latter is a threat of deterrence: 'refrain from doing what I object to, or else'.

The country receiving the threat, or studying the possibility that a threat would be made, considers the evidence that a threat both could be carried out (the capability of the threatener to do what they threaten) and the likelihood that they will do so. Neither are foregone conclusions. Threateners may have the means but not the will, or the will but not the means, or neither.

There is also the possibility that the country being deterred had no intention of behaving in the way that is prescribed by the threatener; there is also the possibility that they intend to behave in the manner prescribed by the threatener, and do not need to be threatened. This creates the possibility that they behave contrary to their intentions in order to demonstrate their immunity from threats, which is hardly the intention of the threatener in the first place.

Threats once made have a momentum about them: if challenged, the threatener has the choice of carrying out the threat (and taking the consequences), or of backing off (and losing credibility). Some threats are inevitably implemented where the threatener has the capability of carrying them through, with dire consequences. The more specific the threat, the more difficult it is to back off. Credibility is not lightly sacrificed. The more vague the threat, the less credible it is as an instrument of compliance or as a deterrent. It is often easier to start a war than stop one.

States increase the credibility of their threats by establishing their commitment. The more inevitable their response, the more committed they appear, and therefore the less likely they are to have to implement their threat. The problem is that the more committed they are, the more specific they have to be to the action they will take, if certain well defined steps are threatening. But the more specific they are — 'any incursions into our territory will be resisted by all means at our disposal' — the less room for manoeuvre they have. Two drunken soldiers stumbling across the border could start a war.

Pure coercion does not require a threat to be implemented. If the other country complies or is deterred without having to implement a threat, then the exercise is more than satisfied: In industrial relations, a similar situation operates. If the implicit, though not necessarily explicit, threat of a strike forces the management to make an offer that is within the union's settlement range, the company has been coerced by its own perceptions of the consequences of failing to move towards the union's expected position. This is also seen in commercial negotiating, when managers refrain from a course of action which they would otherwise choose, because somebody raises the question of what the competition will do if they act in that way.

12.9 Peace negotiations

Wars (and strikes) are easier to start than to stop. There are immense problems in ending them, particularly when neither side can strike a knock-out blow. Sometimes the opportunities for ending a war are missed; a country in a winning position, presses its advantage rather than sues for peace, and being unable to crush the enemy ends up with a stalemate. Likewise, the country in a losing position, but unwilling to negotiate

170

peace from a position of weakness, refuses to negotiate a peace, and hangs on until exhausted or a change in the fortunes of war materializes.

How does a country signify its willingness to resort to negotiation? If it believes it is winning, it may fear that an overture to the other side would convince it that resistance is worthwhile; if it believes it is losing, it may fear that an overture would encourage the other side to press its military advantage. Terminating a war is problematic because any move for peace risks being misinterpreted both by the other side, and by one's own forces ('why risk my life in military valour if the Generals are talking peace?').

Bringing fighting factions to the negotiating table is extremely difficult. Tensions are bound to be high. Each may wish peace, but be wary of misinterpretation of its motives. Indeed, it may make loud noises about not needing to talk peace, but 'if you want to do so, we are willing to listen'. This puts the other side on their guard, and they are likely to avow that it is 'not we who are needing to talk peace, but if you want to do so, we are happy to listen to your proposals'. Both sides refuse to take responsibility for their actions, and each tries to shift the onus of seeking peace onto the other. Naturally, not a few of the early meetings between combatant sides (in wars and strikes) end up in failure, each blaming the other for misleading them about their intentions.

Experienced negotiators know that these early failures on peace talks are inevitable. Neither wishes to undermine the sacrifices of its fighting forces. But negotiate they must to end the war. The early tense meetings give way to longer negotiations on matters of substance. Most peace negotiations take longer than anticipated, and have pacifistic effects on the troops ('why die today, if we are to be at peace tomorrow?').

In strikes, failure of the negotiations, could cause a break in the ranks of the strikers and start 'back to work' movements which undermine the union's position in the peace talks, and, with aggressive managements, encourage them to take a harder line in the hope that further rejection will send more men back to work and make the peace talks redundant. Hence, timing peace talks is critical to the outcome of the war or strike. The side that has reserves (fresh fighting troops, solidarity support in crucial areas) can best ride out disappointment. If a side has no reserves at all, it has probably sued for peace at an inopportune moment.

In general, the country with the least to fear from prolonged warfare has the most bargaining power at the negotiations. This need not mean the country with the most economic or military strength. It is the country with the most to lose by continuing the war, not the country that has the most. A poorer country could have more to lose from losing the war than a richer country. This could give it sufficient edge for it to continue the war, or be willing to do so, and force the other country into negotiations.

12.10   Closing stages

Closing the final gap between two sides at the international level involves more than just exchanging final concessions. Negotiations take place in public as has been noted. If neither side has gone public in the argument stage there is every chance they will do so towards the end of the negotiations, particularly if they are trying to set the other side up as the cause of a 'breakdown' or they are trying to influence the other side's perceptions of their own commitment to some point to encourage them to make the final concessions.

The difficulties this publicity causes are not to be exaggerated but they can be serious. Near the end of the negotiation the final shape of the agreement is becoming apparent. Politicians often change their minds, or events take place which cause them to revalue their benefits from the likely agreement. Accusations of 'bad faith', etc., can actually increase as the point of agreement is approached. Minor disagreements, or apparent sticking to a position, can be interpreted as provocative and aimed at forcing a breakdown. You would do well to work to the following rule in observing the closing stage of an international negotiation: if one party announces that agreement is close, discount it — they are trying to put pressure on the other side to close the gap (it is likely that it is they who are being stubborn); if one party announces a breakdown is imminent, discount it — they are similarly trying to put pressure on the other side (perhaps threatening a breakdown over some minor issue when in fact agreement is imminent).

NEVER IS NOT A SIGNAL

Relationships between France and New Zealand were strained in the aftermath of the 'Rainbow Warrior' affair. Two French agents were jailed for ten years for participation in the sinking of the Greenpeace ship and the death of a crew member.

New Zealand was adamant that the agents would serve their sentences in full. France worked for their release and linked their release to French use of its EEC veto when New Zealand agricultural exports came up for review. The United Nations Secretary-General mediated. When New Zealand announced that it would 'never release the agents to freedom', most commentators latched on to the word 'never'. Experienced negotiators noted the signal words 'to freedom'. The agents were released six weeks later to a French Pacific island.

---

13 Strategy and Tactics

13.1 Introduction

Strategy is the game plan you use to achieve your objectives. Tactics are the individual elements of your game plan. Gambits are 'try-ons' and manoeuvres, usually ascribed to your opponent's tactics. In this chapter we discuss some of the more common tactics and gambits used in negotiations. We have resisted the temptation to elaborate with highly complex and subtle negotiating ploys, preferring to end the book as we began it: as a guide to the negotiations practising managers are likely to participate in or observe.

If we assume that your objective in negotiation is to secure an agreement with your opponent on an issue, then the negotiations are really about finding which agreement, of the ones available to you, is most acceptable to both parties. If agreement is not possible the negotiations will make that apparent sooner or later.

This leaves open the question of how to secure the best possible agreement. There is a range of agreements available to both sides which will satisfy them — this is implied by the notion of an overlap in the parties' limit positions. Arriving at a satisfactory agreement is not quite the same as reaching the best possible agreement. In multi-issue negotiations there must be a larger number of potentially satisfactory agreements than there is with a single-issue negotiation, if only because the alternative combinations of maximum gains on one issue and satisfactory gains on another — perhaps even losses on a few issues — are more numerous than there are issues in dispute.

How you play your negotiating moves, and respond to your opponent's moves, will determine in what part of your negotiating range you settle on individual items: at your limit, at your ideal or some position between them.

In preparation you must choose how much movement to allow between your opening offer and your limit. This negotiating margin is a strategic decision. Your tactics will follow from that decision. We can offer the following thoughts on selecting your negotiating margin but they are necessarily, and deliberately, general. A large part of this exercise calls for judgement on your part. First we will consider the power balance.

13.2 The power balance

A deciding factor in your preparation must be the balance of power existing between you and your opponent when you negotiate the issues in dispute. Broadly, the more powerful your position, the smaller your negotiating margin needs to be. In the extreme you can adopt a 'one offer only' stance, which inevitably precludes a negotiating margin. Either he accepts or rejects the offer. If he is strong enough he can impose a one offer only condition on you, forcing you to go to your 'best price' if you want to get an agreement, because you know he is not going to negotiate with you on any implicit margin. If you are competing with other suppliers on a one offer only basis you must be at a disadvantage compared to having the opportunity to negotiate.

Negotiations presuppose that neither party has absolute power. This does not mean that they have equal power. Your opponent may have enough power to cause you to settle nearer your limit but not enough to force you to surrender. He may act under the impression that he has sufficient power — or permit you to suffer the illusion that he has — when in fact he has not. Estimating your own and your opponent's bargaining power can be a highly subjective exercise, open to wide error. Thus the importance of proper preparation and the search for intelligence about your opponent.

Your power increases if the costs of *not* reaching a settlement hurt your opponent more than they hurt you. If buyers are queuing up to buy your product you are in a more powerful position than if you are queuing up with your competitors to sell it. If the costs to you from not getting a deal with your opponent are greater than the costs to you of the deal on his terms you are in a relatively weaker position than he is. Estimating these relative strengths cannot be much more than a guestimate (he might know something you do not).

Some of the information about the relative needs to secure a deal are obvious to the parties. Production deadlines where the loss of the entire production is at stake (newspapers, oil rig construction projects for the North Sea) place the company in a weak position if the labour force chooses to exercise their power, which they often do.

The stronger you feel, the narrower the margin between your ideal and your limit which you are likely to select and the greater your commitment to your opening position. The weaker you feel the wider the margin and the weaker your commitment. In the extreme you will settle for whatever terms you can get (for example, the Russians at the Brest-Litovsk armistice negotiations in 1917 and the Germans at Versailles in 1918).

13.3 One offer only

Major buyers, such as governments, take advantage of their buying power and enforce a system known as tendering. This has the ostensible purpose of ensuring probity in the financial transactions between public servants and commercial enterprises. Under tendering, the lowest bid to supply or the highest to buy, all things being equal, is accepted. The bid is a fixed offer. Negotiating is excluded, particularly when the tender is received at arm's length — in a sealed package opened at an appointed time. Parties submitting tenders are compelled (if collusion is prohibited) to go straight to their 'best price'. They have no room for a negotiating margin.

It is often felt that sealed-bid tendering precludes the possibility of negotiating. In practice the negotiations precede the formal tendering process: it is the specification which is negotiated.

There are two practical dangers in this system. Firstly, when the buyer receives the bids and then attempts to negotiate the successful one downwards, he faces the prospect next time round of the bids being increased to include a negotiating margin. This defeats the purpose of sealed-bid tendering. Secondly, when the buyer does not negotiate on his specification and merely sets out his requirements as if they all had equal priority, the bidder is then faced with a list of unweighted demands and must assume they all have equal importance to the buyer. His tender has to be drawn up as if this was true. It often happens that some of the most expensive items are of marginal importance compared to others but, not knowing this, the tenderer submits a price much higher than would be necessary if he had been able to negotiate on the specification.

SEALED-BID COUNTER

In Scotland houses are sold by sealed tender. The vendor's solicitor asks for 'offers over £X,000 by Friday midday'.

This is a very good system for the seller as he receives offers at or close to the buyers' limits. He sometimes frightens off potential bidders who, while ready to bid a reasonable price, do not bother because they believe others will beat them. If nobody bids in these circumstances, the seller must start over again.

Buyers sometimes place a time-limit on his offer (known as Pre-emptive Bidding'). 'I offer £X + 2 thousand open to acceptance by Wednesday 10 a.m.' This is an attempt to create uncertainty in the vendor. 'If I allow this offer to lapse will I get a better one from someone else.'

The state of the market will dictate the efficiency of this tactic.

If a party feels it is in a strong position it uses a similar strategy: it adopts one offer only and refuses to negotiate any movement. It is effectively price-making and forcing the other party to price-take, or leave it.

Ford of England used a similar strategy in a pay 'negotiation' some years ago. They made the unions an offer and announced they would not improve on it. The unions called a strike but it crumbled when the men learned what the company's opening (and closing) offer was. This had been carefully selected by the company to be high enough to attract most employees who would prefer to take a relatively high sum (compared to previous years) without a strike than lose money in a strike trying to improve on it.

13.4 Conflicting strategies

Negotiating presupposes that there is a margin. The parties may not know how big the margin is, whether it is significant or not, whether it is within their settlement range or not, but they expect the other party to have 'padded' their offer to some extent. They do not expect the other party to adopt a non-negotiable stance. If one party has come to negotiate and the other adopts one offer only there is bound to be an incompatibility between their expectations. Sooner or later the party willing to negotiate will be forced to revise its perception of the nature of the 'negotiations'. It might for a while interpret the other party's behaviour as an ultra-firm commitment to its opening position but eventually it will realize that it is a one offer only bid. Predictably, accusations of 'bad faith' will be made.

If both parties adopted one offer only there would be deadlock if the offers did not overlap, which would be the case if the parties choose opening offers close to their ideal (excluding the extremely unlikely circumstance that the parties' ideals overlap). If a party's one offer only is inside the other party's limit it may be that a deal is possible, providing the party moving second does not revise its ideal and move its one offer only further away. In general one offer only is a high-risk strategy: it courts total rejection (perhaps letting the competition in) and it risks settling on worse terms than you could have negotiated.

Nobody likes to be offered something on an 'or else' basis, which is what one offer only is in effect. Only extreme power or extreme weakness makes one offer only a viable, or necessary, strategy.

Negotiating is about removing the padding on the opposition's proposals. The gambits and tactics of negotiation are aimed at achieving this overall goal. The reason why negotiators hesitate to commit themselves is because they can never be sure that they have squeezed their opponent's margin as far as it will go. They also like to settle at a position short of their own limit. This encourages them to settle earlier rather than later. A knowledge of tactics helps them achieve this.

YESTERDAY'S TOP DOGS

A major photocopier manufacturer held patents on his machine. His policy was to rent not to sell. As long as the machine had a technical advantage he maintained his rental-only policy. When the advantage disappeared because of rival technology he was forced to negotiate sales as well as rentals. The balance of power had shifted and he had to learn new skills.

Oil companies used to preferentially treat large consumers of their products. Since 1986, with the fall in crude oil prices, oil has become much less scarce. Now the major suppliers actively seek to sell at whatever price they can get.

Tin-can manufacturing used to require a certain expertise possessed by a small number of companies. New production technology simplified production methods — anyone with the right machinery could make cans. The traditional manufacturers are having to negotiate can sales against much wider competition.

13.5 Common gambits and tactics

It is not, of course, possible to cover every single gambit or tactic which you are likely to come across in the course of your negotiations. The variants are almost infinite. There is no end to the surprises possible at the negotiating table.

However, there is a relatively small number of standard gambits and tactics which occur with sufficient frequency to make it worth your while to study and think about them in quiet moments. If you already negotiate regularly you will recognize most of what we have selected. [The authors would be delighted to hear from readers on the variants you have experienced, or indeed, others you think should be included. Our selection is bound to be subjective. This chapter could have been many times longer but space and balance required a fairly ruthless cutting.]

We have laid out the selected gambits and tactics in the form we thought would be most helpful for readers to recognize and assimilate. We use direct speech to illustrate the most common form used by negotiators, or, where appropriate, a statement summarizing the tactic. We give our views of the negotiating purpose of the illustrated tactic and occasionally one or two examples of its possible use in the world at large. A suggestion or two follows on how you might respond, or expect your opponent to respond, if one of you brings the tactic into play. Note that we use dots (. . .) where the specific issue in the negotiations is referred to by the speaker. There is no particular significance in the order we have set them out. Broadly, they follow the order of a negotiation from opening to close but this is not strictly adhered to where the exposition benefits from bringing individual elements together.

Shot gun

'Unless you agree immediately to . . . we are not prepared to discuss anything else.' (Often accompanied by a sanction threat.)

Your opponent is attempting to force you to give up some

position you have so as to weaken your ability to use that position to extract concessions from him in the areas you are about to negotiate. This is used frequently in dismissal cases ('reinstate before talks'); where stoppages have occurred ('we will not negotiate under duress'); insistence on a pre-condition for negotiation where a major principle is at stake ('no negotiation with Arab States unless and until they recognize the existence of the State of Israel' — 'no negotiations with Israel unless and until they recognize the rights of the Palestinians to self-determination').

Your response is conditioned by the balance of power. Are they strong enough to enforce their demands? If not, keep them talking either about the inequity of making unreasonable preconditions or the benefits of discussing the issue rather than jeopardize mutual interests.

Off-limits

In formal relationships it is not uncommon for the parties to specify the extent and the nature of the limits they agree to adhere to. For example, in the case of the Engineering Employers' Federation and the Engineering Unions, an agreement was made in 1922 to define the limits of their relationship and the agreement that was made (known somewhat incorrectly as the 'York Memorandum') lasted to the 1970s. In the agreement the following principle was stated:

> 'Employers have the right to manage their establishments and the trade unions have the right to exercise their functions.'

This was of tremendous significance because it overshadowed all the negotiations between both sides. Originally it was interpreted to mean that an employer could make whatever changes he wanted in the workshop arrangements without consultation with the workforce and if they criticized or objected to the new arrangements they had to take them up through the procedure laid down for resolving (or as the agreement put it, 'avoiding') disputes.

In other words, the employees had to work the *'status quo'* and negotiate a return to the *'status quo ante'*. This caused enormous trouble as the balance of shop floor power changed towards the unions in the 1960s, who insisted that the *'status quo'* must be defined as the previous situation and that the employer could not make changes without going through procedure first. The inability to agree on this new interpretation contributed to the eventual ending of the agreement. In the 1980s the balance of power had shifted back to the employers. While the original agreement was not re-introduced, many employees operated as if its central division of roles continued.

It is not uncommon to hear an 'off-limits' gambit of the following type:

> 'We are certainly prepared to discuss the criteria used in staff promotion but we are not prepared to countenance any discussions on named individuals nor act in any way which undermines the absolute right of the management to decide upon promotion.'

Or:

> 'The issue of . . . is, as far as we are concerned, non-negotiable.' (Often accompanied by a reference to the items that are negotiable.)

Your opponent may be telling you he prefers to break-off rather than negotiate on the 'sacred' issue. Much the same as the previous case applies. If they have the strength they will prevail, if not it becomes negotiable. They might be signalling the possibility of concessions on the other items in dispute. You may commit yourself not to raise the 'sacred' issue in order to get progress on the other items; you may want to do that so as not to prejudice your rights to raise the issue at some other time ('without prejudice' is a useful phrase in negotiations).

Try: 'Lets leave that to one side, while we discuss the other issues'. This does not endorse 'off limits' but it neutralizes it for the moment. Examples are likely to be found wherever one party regards the other party as solemnly bound to it by obligation or contract or moral position. ('We do not negotiate with terrorists'; 'liability is not negotiable'; 'debts can be re-scheduled but not abrogated'.)

'It gives me no pleasure to be here under these circumstances but I have been instructed to try once more to reach a settlement. I have some proposals which I suggest you consider very carefully because if you act unreasonably I will be just as happy to resolve this dispute by the other means open to me.'

This might be a genuine last ditch attempt to come to a settlement in an atmosphere of mutual hostility. The speaker might also be spoiling for a fight.

In recent negotiations in El Salvador between the government and the insurgents, each has expressed its desire for a negotiated peace, but each has also declared their willingness, if necessary, and with regret, to continue the civil war if the other side does not make large concessions.

The fact that they negotiated at all suggests that the more bellicose rhetoric could be discounted but the potential threat to break off negotiations could not be entirely dismissed. Discriminating between stance-making and genuine commitment to the alternative of sanctions is essential if you are to avoid either being intimidated into major (and unnecessary) concessions or provoking yourself, or the others, into demonstrating what they are threatening to do. Likewise, it is essential to separate what you need to state to underline your credibility from what you may be tempted into overstating thus risking the calling of your bluff.

Tough guy — nice guy

Your opponent opens with a very hard line on the issue in front of you both. He might also allude to sanction threats ('the men won't stand for it', 'they are chaffing at the bit'). He is followed by another member of his team (sometimes he plays both roles himself) who puts forward a more reasonable view in comparison with the first speaker, though his 'reasonable' may still be unacceptable to you. He will also tend to give assurances about handling the problems previously alluded to ('I think we can persuade the lads to calm down if we get this settled satisfactorily').

This is one of the oldest gambits in the business. It is also one of the most regularly successful, if it is done right. But it has risks for the user. If the tough guy part is overdone it may provoke rather then intimidate. If nice guy comes in too early he may increase the opponent's confidence because the scripted softening of the attitude might be interpreted as a response to the opponent's reaction to the tough guy perform-ance. This encourages the opponent to resist instead of crumble.

The tough guy part is often played to establish a high negotiating platform, thus creating negotiating room for nice guy. An example of this can be illustrated from a recent negotiation in the construction industry between the main contractor and a sub-contractor supplying air conditioning equipment. The tough guy part was played by the main contractor's managing director who told the sub-contractor what he was about to do:

'We have been badly let down by you and your engineers. This has caused me to review our entire operation with you. I have instructed my site manager to report in detail to me on the specification discrepancies in your delivery and installation work. My contracts people are now in discussion with other suppliers to see what they can do for us quickly to replace your equipment. Your personnel are being flown home on Saturday and stage payments have been stopped. I intend to place contracts with these companies if they can guarantee quality and if our talks today fail to produce something satisfactory. We will go public on the reasons why we have had to make these changes and certainly the client will be left in no doubt. I hold you responsible for these failings and the consequent costs, and frankly I do not care how much it costs us to put it right because you will be sued anyway. I'm in no mood for new excuses.'

This tough guy line was followed, later in the negotiations, by a nice guy approach from the contractor's projects manager:

'Our main interest is in completing our contracts, not in suing suppliers. But you have to convince me that it is going to be sorted out. I'll put my engineers to work with your chaps to test and run the equipment. You will have to cover the site costs and replacement effort but if you can come up with a special effort I will get our side to hold off from taking irreversible steps. If you come up with an answer we will put behind us this unfortunate experience.'

Two hours later agreement was reached, the main contractor dropped his claims and the sub-contractor paid only for the additional work.

Russian Front

This is an adaptation of the previous gambit using alternative proposals instead of alternative presentation styles. Your opponent is offered two choices, one of them worse (for him) than the other. He is intimidated to accept the other in order to avoid the horrific proposal. ('Anything, but don't send me to the Russian Front'). Its chances of success depend upon the credibility of the alternatives.

An opponent may introduce a proposal which is totally unacceptable to you but which you believe he has every intention of forcing you to consider implementing. For example, a management backed off from revising a sick-pay scheme they operated but which had overshot its budget through short-term absenteeism because the union side began to raise the issue of an attendance bonus. This proposal was anathema to them so they considered themselves 'lucky' to have 'escaped' from it by a compromise which actually did nothing to halt the absenteeism. They had been 'Russian Fronted'.

You can handle this gambit either by using 'Off-limits' or remembering it takes two to agree that and if you do not agree with a proposal, it remains a proposal. You can also counter his extreme alternatives with equally extreme alternatives for him. This can lead to a mutual movement to more reasonable negotiating ground by a mutual withdrawal of the extreme alternatives by both of you.

A television rental company succeeded in obtaining part of

185

A docker's union in Sydney used the tough guy–nice guy gambit with great success for many years. Here the performances were almost theatrical and relied heavily on the established reputations of the local union leaders as men who preferred a dispute to a compromise. They worked the gambit this way: one of the union negotiating team was instructed never to say anything at the negotiations. He was told simply to stare at the management people with enthusiastic aggression and to nod furiously when his own side made militant speeches. But whenever one of his own side showed any signs of compromise by signalling a modification of the union's position on something, he was instructed to turn his attention onto the union man and with glares, grunts and mild cursing, he was to pretend to be getting very annoyed at his colleague's concessionary behaviour. This was acted out in public in front of the management. It enabled the union leaders conducting the negotiations to demonstrate their willingness to compromise and the reasons why they were unable to do so. If they made any moves towards the management position they were at risk from the 'militants'. Indeed, to underline this occasionally, the 'tough guy' sometimes increased his cursing from mild to heavy, even making a physical lunge at the 'compromiser' (but held back, of course, by the men next to him!). This invariably had the desired effect.

The management when making any proposal would tend to look at the reaction of the tough guy as their guide to the acceptability of the proposal. If he looked fierce and began to murmur they would tend to back off, if he looked impassive and perhaps indifferent they would tend to continue. He completed his image-building role by only one speech consisting of one sentence at any meeting: 'Pull them out!', i.e. go on strike. For this he became famous and was called the 'dentist'. The employers believed in him absolutely and it is probable he came eventually to believe in himself too.

a hotel chain's business. They had considerably undercut their competitors' price to gain this foothold but then found that they were suffering an abnormally high maintenance cost on their sets.

Analysis showed that the hotels they were supplying with TV sets were at the lower end of the hotel chain's range. The contract for the more up-market hotels in the chain was up for renewal and the TV company wanted to extend its business with the chain. They were faced with the problem of low profitability on their existing business and a low price precedent for any new business.

Securing a straight price increase was likely to prove unpopular and they adopted a 'Russian Front' strategy. They explained their problem with the unforeseen maintenance costs to the hotel chain and presented a number of options for dealing with it which were selected by them for their general unattractiveness or impracticality. After prolonged discussion the hotel chain suggested an increased price per set rental as a better solution. The TV company agreed and proceeded to negotiate the increase.

Aim high — aim low

This gambit is similar to the 'Russian Front' but this time you do not get an alternative offered. Your opponent opens with an extremely high demand, much more than you had budgeted for. You are faced with the choice of withdrawing or matching him in some way. His gambit is aimed at enticing you into a much higher offer than you would otherwise have contemplated, which you might do if you believe his commitment to a high demand is firm. By taking an extreme position he moves you closer to his real ideal. Exactly similar considerations apply if your opponent comes in at a very low figure in a purchase deal.

If you withdraw he might apply sanctions. You will have to resist or revise your position. If your withdrawal damages him more than it does you, he will have to revise his position. That is a risk for him. You could also come in very low to match his very high opening. Instead of revising your limit towards him you revise your ideal away from him.

House clearers usually make very low nominal offers for a house full of furniture. In most cases the sellers assume that this is the market price and agree. The buyer has an air of indifference about him, long cultivated. He removes the furniture and sells it at a higher price. If he offered a 'reasonable' price you would probably haggle and seek other quotes. His shock tactic mostly works.

Sell cheap, get famous

> 'We are not pretending that the offer we have made meets you on price but the real pay-off for you will come from the image your company will gain from being an endorsed supplier of goods to a multi-million pound international company. Think what having us on your client list will do for your future sales.'

This is one of the major 'come-ons' in the negotiating business. It is used at all levels and in all walks of life. Firms do not advertise jobs with low wages — they talk about 'good prospects' instead; buyers talk about possible 'future orders' which the supplier will have a chance of competing for; television producers raise expectations of a 'series' or 'world rights' and so on. Sometimes it is true; these things happen. If you believe them you will accept. But most of the time you should recognize it for what it is: a gambit to get you to sell something cheaply. If you are 16 years old, a new salesman or an unknown playwright you may have little choice. You can test the reality of the prospects by asking for specific details and commitments.

Who's your friend?

This gambit aims to prevent you doing something because of the alleged bad publicity you will attract ('Do you want to be known as the only employer around here who does not have a children's Christmas party?'; 'Your PR department will have kittens when they hear what you are trying to introduce'; 'Do you really want to be known as the bank that forecloses on little old widowed ladies?'). It can be powerfully persuasive stuff, particularly if you have a guilty conscience. Publicity can be damaging; if it is controversial it may antagonize one group (who may not buy your products anyway) and enthuse another group who do. A major car manufacturer in England refused to re-instate a dismissed employee who had been caught sleeping on the night shift, on the grounds that to do so would make them the laughing stock of British industry.

Salami

Salami comes in thin slices. It is not eaten in one go. This is the intention of this particular tactic. It is suggested when something unpalatable is being proposed. By offering to introduce the arrangement a bit at a time and over a relatively long period it is hoped that there will be less resistance from those affected. It works too. Managements offer to 'phase in' new methods. They agree to allow 'natural wastage' rather than compulsory redundancy. Sales staff try for a little of a company's business if they are having trouble getting in against an established supplier — they may begin by asking for a right to quote for some orders, hoping that once they get something in, other orders will follow. Unions gradually extend their involvement with managerial decisions, gradually introduce more restrictive methods of work and gradually work towards a 'closed shop'. American diplomats assert that the Russians are adept at using Salami tactics.

The following chronology of events illustrates the Salami tactic at work:

January 1986 The union recognized as the appropriate body for individuals to be represented in disciplinary and grievance cases.

June 1987 Recognition extended to allow union to represent groups in wage negotiations.

CONTINUING RELATIONSHIPS

When one of the authors joined the industrial relations department of a major car manufacturing plant in the 1960s a simple lesson in the conventions of industrial relations as practised in that plant was taught him by an experienced senior shop steward.

'You will understand the set-up here', he said, 'once you realize that the rule is: when you need cars, we screw you and when you can't sell the naffing cars you screw us'.

Negotiations conducted to win short-term 'victories' over an opponent regardless of the future relationship eventually come home to roost — the particular car plant has since closed.

February 1988 Company agrees to advise all new employees that union is the appropriate body to represent them in the company's procedure agreements and that the company has no objections to them joining the union. Company also states it has no objections to employees not being members of the union.

December 1988 Company agrees that all employees in the grades covered by the union will operate under the negotiated agreements and that no individual arrangements will be made for non-members.

November 1989 Company signs 100 per cent union membership agreement and requires all employees on joining the company to join the union as a condition of employment. Established employees exempted on a conscience clause.

November 1990 Full closed shop agreed and all employees, new or established, obliged to join union as a condition of employment; persons leaving the union, or expelled, will be

190

dismissed. Tight conscience clause inserted only for established employees with long service in the company.

Next steps Removal of the exemption clause for established employees on conscience grounds. Requirement that all suppliers are unionized. Requirement that supervisory grades join the white-collar section of the union. Option of union membership to management grades.

Apart from the policy issues, which we are not concerned with here, the negotiator faced with the Salami tactic has to decide upon the implications of what is being proposed by the opponent. He can influence the rate of concessions and the extent. A 'defensive' strategy would aim to bind every concession with as many qualifications and exemptions as possible and to use these in future negotiations. It is inexcusable to be the 'victim' of the Salami tactic unwittingly; it is necessary to use it when circumstances dictate it to be appropriate.

The 'mandate' demand

Management negotiators are frequently faced with a 'mandate' demand. This is usually stated in the form: 'The lads have instructed me to get . . . and we are *mandated* not to go back to them until we get it'.

To illustrate how to cope with such a demand consider this example from a wage negotiation on behalf of production control supervisors in an electronics factory. Negotiations on a 12-month salary deal had deadlocked at an offer of £295 per week basic, plus immediate shift allowance improvements increasing these payments from £1.70 an hour to £1.80 an hour. The wage deal, if accepted, was to run from 1 January to 31 December. The union's 'mandate' demand was for a minimum of £300 per week. Management preparation and intelligence confirmed the strength of feeling surrounding the mandate. The inexperienced negotiator or the 'split-the-difference' pundit would attempt to influence and negotiate a compromise at £297.50. The negotiator experienced in bargaining would see it differently. He would ask himself: 'How can I repackage this deal to make it more acceptable now that I know the union's 'MUST GET' position of £300 a week? How can I help the union to sell the deal to their members?' The company reconstructed its offer, at the same total cost as its opening offer, like this:

Salary: £295 from 1 January 1987 for 3 months
             £300 from 1 April 1987 for a further 12 months
Shift allowance: £1.72 from 1 January 1987
                      £1.75 from 1 July 1987
                      £1.80 from 1 January 1987

This new package allowed the union negotiators to report to the members that the mandate had been satisfied. The company negotiators achieved:

A deal at the same total cost.
A 15-month agreement.
A resolution of the negotiations.

The production controllers achieved:

Their £300 per week demand within three months.
The same shift allowance improvements within the total term of this agreement as originally offered.

The 'disguised' claim

A favourite area for 'disguised' claims is the Health and Safety Act. Some cynics have suggested that the difference between a safe working practice and an unsafe working practice is about £2.00 per hour.

The argument step would go something like this: 'This section of the factory is absolutely freezing for much of the winter. It is dangerous for men to be working in these conditions with moving machinery operating and all of the men with numb fingers. We are considering calling in the Factory Inspectors, etc. . . . Some of our members have gone out at their own expense and bought fur-lined boots and thick sweaters so that they can put in a fair day's work for the company. It really is not good enough and you are going to have to do something about it.'

The union could not ask directly for concessionary clothing

192

allowances. They would have to admit, if they did, that an allowance was more important than the temperature in the machine shop. However, if the management negotiators wished to pick the issue up, there is an obvious area for bargaining.

Brooklyn optician

There are two ways this tactic can be used: one to raise the price and the other to increase what you get for a specific price. The first application can be illustrated by the technique used by a Brooklyn optician to get extra cash from customers:
'The lenses you require for your eye condition come in at $10 (pause) each. Frames will cost you $15 (pause) plus $10 fitting for the basic model which is good enough if you don't let anybody see you wearing them. The dress models come in at $25 (pause) fitting $15. If you want the work done in five days it will cost $10 (pause) a day (pause); weekend work is an extra $10 (pause) a day. Regular black frames are $5 and coloured ones $8. Rimless come in at $20 (pause) and $15 if you want gold (pause) leaf. Solid gold is $80 (pause) for each lens frame (pause); moving parts are an extra $10 (pause) each. . . .'
The optician is building up his final price by charging something for any variable he can think of. He is pausing because he is giving the customer a chance to close and for as long as the customer refrains from doing so he will go on, no doubt charging for delivery and insurance, and possible personal home fitting (extra for an assistant!).

This add-on tactic can be used in reverse by a customer. First he establishes the basic price and then adds-on extras, keeping the price the same:
'How much do you charge for bed and breakfast?'
'£75 a day.'
'If you will agree to provide dinner as well I will agree to stay for two weeks' (*pause to get agreement*).
'If you will provide lunch as well I will agree to sharing a room with my children.'

193

Polite impertinence

You want to unnerve your creditor by coolly implying you have more power than he has. If he is intimidated by your air of confidence he will assume he is in the weaker position.

'Your overdraft facility is now due for review. Please contact me to arrange an appointment to discuss the matter.' (*Reply*): 'I am pleased to have the opportunity of discussing the progress of my business and would be happy to see you in my office at 11.10 am on the 3rd of next month.'

Noah's Ark

This is so-called because it came in about that time and has been running the rounds ever since. 'You will have to do much better than the price you have put up. I have proposals' (usually tapping a plain file on his desk) 'from your competitors which offer me much better terms.' Every commercial negotiator (and junior salesman) will have heard that one time and time again. It is almost always a bluff. If he has better terms he has no need to negotiate with you anyway. It is more likely that he has lower priced quotes for inferior products and he is attempting to frighten you into conceding a lower price for yours. He might also be using competing quotes to drive them both down (he will immediately inform your competitor that your price is now below his and 'would he like to requote', etc.). Three possible counters:

1   Counter bluff: 'Then I would advise you to accept them'.
2   Call his bluff: 'If you are asking me to match another quote you will need to show it to me to ensure we are not comparing apples and pears'.
3   Take the initiative: 'I assume that you are saying that you prefer my proposals but wish me to justify my price?'

Dutch auction (a variation of Noah's Ark)

Two British companies selling an identical industrial chemical (liquid nitrogen) were competing for a customer's

194

business. A Dutch auction ensued, each company successively undercutting the other. The outcome of this was that one company eventually tabled a very low bid which was immediately matched by the other. The first company then withdrew its bid leaving their competitors to take the business at a tiny profit.

To avoid this situation arising again the 'unsuccessful' company adopted a policy of 'bid last'. 'Are you in a position to come to a decision today Mr Seller?'. 'No, I still have some more work to do on our proposal — I am sure that you will find it extremely attractive. May I suggest that you obtain my competitor's best price so that you can see how my proposals compare.'

Veiled threats

Threats of sanctions can be very risky. They raise the emotional temperature. 'Are you threatening me?' is a sure sign that what you have said has been taken in an antagonistic way. 'Of course not' is your expected reply. If you had intended to warn them of the consequences of what they are leading themselves towards, your disavowal weakens the impact of your message. But if your message is seen as a threat, it weakens the corrective purpose behind you making it: presumably you do not want them to do what you are warning them against.

There are two useful ways of using a sanction threat effectively:

1   'The consequences of our not agreeing are these. . . . However, as neither of us want that let us see what we can do to avoid it.' ('How do you like our new electric chair? Of course, we hope we will never have to use it?')

2   In this version you make the sanction credible. 'We, of course, may not require this component. Our engineers are currently investigating an alternative method which appears to be marginally cheaper.' (This last is a version of 'Noah's Ark'.)

Your opponent may be starting off negotiations with you in a position of weakness on some issues. His best approach is to try to link the issues he is weak on with other issues in which he is stronger. 'I am prepared to discuss our slow payment of your invoices if you will discuss the poor quality of some of these components you sent last week.'

An example of this linking tactic can be seen in the negotiations between Britain and its EEC partners in 1984 on the issue of Britain's net contributions to the EEC budget. The British had been trying for several years to have their net contributions reduced but some members did not support this view. Coincidently, the Common Agricultural Policy was close to running out of money and it required the unanimous decision of all members to increase its budget. Britain decided to link the two issues: 'We are prepared to vote for an increase in the CAP budget, if, but only if, you agree to reduce Britain's contributions to the overall EEC budget — otherwise we will withhold our vote on CAP and let the EEC go bust.'

Linking issues in this way strengthened Britain's negotiating platform. By keeping the two issues linked it won major concessions.

Another variant of linking is to link one issue to another and state that together they are not acceptable: 'This clause in the contract at the price you are asking is extremely difficult for me to accept'. If you have chosen the right clause — preferably a non-negotiable item — they are likely to move on the price. If the price is firm they might move on the clause. If they do neither you can try 'add-on': 'Well at that price I would require free parts and labour for the next three years'.

Perry Mason

This involves trying to hang you with 'logic'. Your opponent will ask if you agree that such and such is true. Having secured your 'Yes' because the question is framed to be self-evident, he will then ask you another question, implying that the second follows on from the first. If you say 'Yes' again he then goes on to the third question after which, if you answer affirmatively, he will pronounce you 'guilty':

'Do you agree that a stoppage of work took place?'
'Yes'
'Do you agree that this is in breach of procedure?'
'Yes'
'Why then do you persist in defending unconstitutional stoppages?'

Most often the chain of reasoning he is about to use is obvious and you will balk at answering such leading questions. You might insist that there were exceptional circumstances in any case — which there normally are because he uses this tactic to get you to fall into a trap he has set for you. It follows that using the same tactic yourself is unlikely to be very productive. If he is so dim that he does not see it he ought not to be allowed out after dark.

Widows and orphans

This is so familiar that it qualifies for a pension. The idea is to play on your sympathies by relating the issue in dispute to the alleged impact the situation has, or will have, on particularly unfortunate minorities:

'If you insist on your wage demands, my wife and children will end up in the workhouse.'

'The man you sacked has a widowed grandmother who has just lost her war hero husband and breadwinner; his wife has asthma, his little girl is blind and the dog has rabies. . . .' ('Yes, but he did blow up the factory. . . .')

Doomsday

A more credible version of widows and orphans is used to paint the picture so black that you feel you must accept changes. Often this tactic is overdone by opponents and being non-credible, its impact is undermined. A teachers' union leader, however, described the management position on his wage claim as 'the blackest day in the history of education . . . catastrophic effects on schoolchildren are inevitable. . . .' The management increased their offer by 5 per cent.

Quivering quill

In 1977 the then British Prime Minister, James Callaghan, announced at his party's conference that his Government was about to sign a major shipbuilding construction order with the Polish Government worth almost £100 million. This had the intended political effect on his standing inside the Labour Party. It also made him vulnerable to the quivering quill gambit. Once he had publicly stated his Government's commitment, and therefore prestige, to securing the order he had to deliver the signed order or lose considerable public face. But at the time he made his speech the contracts had not yet been signed.

Accordingly when the British delegation arrived in Poland to sign the final contracts the Poles raised some last-minute issues while their pens were hovering over the contracts. These issues involved more financial concessions by the British, valued it is estimated up to £1 million. The British hastily sought fresh instructions and got them: 'Sign'!

Announcing successful contracts before they are signed can prove expensive. Your opponent only has to withhold signature at the moment of you realising your 'triumph' and he can squeeze something extra from you. Of course, he must not try to overdo the 'squeeze' but even an extra 1 per cent is a lot of money on a contract worth upwards of £100 million.

The best counter to the quivering quill is to avoid it in the first place.

Yes, but . . .

The 'Yes, but . . .' tactic consists of saying in effect: 'Yes, we agree to what you are now offering, but we have this other problem we must get out of the way before we can agree to everything'. The 'other problem' is a new issue not raised up to then. It can be particularly infuriating as a tactic if there has been considerable difficulty in reaching agreement on the issues the other side say 'Yes, but . . .' to and it is here that the main weakness of the tactic is exposed. 'Yes, but' is vulnerable to the receiving party losing patience and pulling out, making allegations as to bad faith and dealing with unserious negotiators.

To avoid the 'Yes, but . . .' tactic make all propositions conditional, get all objections out into the open, and make all packages tentative; then for any new issue that is raised use a 'No, but . . .' in reply: 'No, we cannot agree to the introduction of these new issues into the package at this stage, but, if you insist upon them we are certainly prepared to consider them within the package limits and will make adjustments in what we have already proposed as the basis of a solution'.

Your opponent then faces the prospect, not of new additional major concessions, but a repackaging of what is on the table. This is an entirely different position for him, difficult as it may be for you to enforce it if the new issues are genuinely of major importance (though somebody somewhere has not been doing his homework if new issues keep on appearing). But difficult as they may be it is a superior response to one which keeps rewarding the 'Yes, but . . .' tactic with additional major concessions. If you use 'Yes, but . . .' and your opponent rewards you it is your duty to try again, and again, and perhaps again with the same tactic, until he stops rewarding you. What is true for you is also true for him when he uses 'Yes, but. . . .'

No authority here!

If the person you are negotiating with does not have the authority to settle, you will have a hard time getting agreement before your 'best' proposals are referred elsewhere for a decision. You can take it for granted that the person who does have authority to settle will not be satisfied with your

199

proposals in some respect when their messenger reports on them. If you are keen to settle you will be forced to make additional concessions when the messenger returns with the response.

By not having authority, the negotiator can generate movement off the other side's ideal towards its limits without necessarily having to respond positively. The person who does have authority is not present and is therefore immune to the face-to-face pressures to say 'Yes'. By removing authority to settle from the negotiations, you reserve an option to press for more in order to secure agreement.

For this reason many principals use agents to negotiate for them and reserve the right to apply a final veto themselves. Some negotiators insist on dealing with 'principals only' in order to obviate having a 'yes, but' response to their carefully worked out 'best deal'.

If you must negotiate with an agent, or anybody who requires higher approval, you had better keep something back from your final position otherwise you will be pressed to cross your limits, and not always for small amounts.

If you can insist on dealing only with the organ grinder and not with his monkey, do so if you are prepared to face the tougher pressure of dealing with the people with higher authority. This last ought not to be shrugged off. People who have authority get where they are because they know what they are doing. If you are unsure of yourself, you had better do most of your business with the other guy's 'monkeys' and hope they do not squeeze you too hard!

Above all, find out what authority the other party has before you embark on the bargaining step. It might be too late if you have gone to your limits to achieve your MUST GET positions and then find that they have to get 'board approval' before they sign the agreement.

The Mother Hubbard

If you can simultaneously convince the other party that you want to do business with them but that there is no way that you can meet their opening demands, it is possible that you can use the 'Mother Hubbard' (of 'the cupboard is bare' fame) and get them to reduce their demands, sometimes by significant amounts.

It works like this: they are made to believe that they are close to a deal (you genuinely want to buy their product for instance), when you tell them that try as you might there is just no way that you can meet their price. Naturally, they are not going to believe you just because you tell them this — it is a poor negotiator who does not expect a price objection in a negotiation, if only as a test of his resolve.

The Mother Hubbard requires that you show them evidence of your inability to pay their asking price. You have to show them that the cupboard is indeed bare!

Show them a printed instruction on prices that you can pay. The printed word carries more authority — why is not important — than the spoken word.

Show them your budget total. Show them a written memo requiring you not to go over budget this or next year. Show them an instruction from your boss not to spend more than a certain amount on this particular purchase. There is a very high chance that they will accept what you show them at face value.

When faced with a Mother Hubbard the least you can do is take care not to believe everything you are shown. The so-called written evidence may be a 'creative fake' (used in more than one negotiation!) specially prepared for the meeting using a high speed copier and a word processor.

You should try to find another way of meeting your price — change the package not the price. Offer them alternatives. But beware. The Mother Hubbard is a negotiator's most powerful tool when sprung after careful preparation. It is almost irresistible. Sometimes you do not realise it has been sprung on you until afterwards — we know, for we use it and fall for it regularly!

No can do

Many companies severely constrain their negotiators with a version of 'no authority here'. They devolve authority to settle to their negotiators and then impose on them tight limits of discretion, usually stated in the form of rules and procedures. Certainly, you can get a deal with them, but it will be a deal fairly firmly circumscribed by decisions previously laid down by higher authority.

You press for a discount on your quantity order and they respond with: 'Sorry, no can do. It is against company policy to discount on orders unless they are for at least 100,000 units a month'.

This means you have to take on 'company policy' (whatever that means) to get a discount. Your opponent is in a good psychological position, for he can stand firm without discomfort under the shelter of somebody else's veto on discounts below 100,000 ('It's not me that is saying no, but company policy').

This can be applied right across the board in almost all negotiations. It is always credible to have a policy on something, even if the reasoning behind the policy is more than a trifle obscure. 'Sorry. No can do. My wife/husband would never let me agree to that.'

Every variable can have an arbitrary limit imposed on it. By imposing a policy limit you restrict the demands and thereby perhaps the expectations of the other party. People are more prepared to accept less if they are convinced it is the best they can do and if what stops them getting more is something called company policy. Do not underestimate the need to save face in your opponent. He may be upset if he believes that it is your intransigence alone that stops him getting a concession on something, but he will be much more relaxed at not getting his way if he believes that you are bound by company rules that restrict your discretion. (And, let's be clear here, the reason why companies restrict the discretion of their negotiators is precisely to bolster their resistance to demands from the likes of you that otherwise they might find difficult to resist).

Really large organizations have immense credibility when their negotiators introduce policy limits and use 'no can do'. The larger the organization the less impressive your bit of business compared to their turnover.

If they have a strict thirty day credit limit, an automatic

reference back to the board on business over £100,000, a standard performance bond system, a minimum/maximum pricing, ordering, delivery, storage, or returns policy, a myriad of committees and procedures that must be respected, and a host of other restrictions (especially if they are in print), there is not a lot you can do about it unless you are very determined, or you are very important to them.

At this point we make two points to comfort you if faced with 'no can do'. First, negotiators know that mounting a credible assault on 'company/union/government policy' is very difficult and therefore if you do decide to take it on it says a lot about your resolve. In this case 'no can do' tests your resolve. If you crumble to a 'no can do' clearly you had none!

Secondly, negotiators in small organizations have the most discretion, in that you are likely to be dealing with the person who has authority or someone close to him or her. Where discretion exists you can negotiate past 'company policy' to get a deal.

In the case of large organizations, where company policy is likely to be spelled out in detail, you need not despair of taking on a 'no can do'. The larger the organization the less visible the individual deals that its hundreds or thousands of negotiators sign up each year. 'One offs' trump 'no can dos'. The manager concerned can 'lose' the 'one off' deal with you that breaches company policy without a lot of flak if you persist in not being intimidated by the 'no can do' when you hear it.

'Sure, I can see why you require a minimum order level for your suppliers to qualify for a discount and I have no doubt that the majority of them willingly accept this. However, my order level today is a one-off situation which, as we build up our relationship over the years, will more than be recovered by you in the total orders we can put through your company. For this, I require the bulk discount applied to all my orders.'

If negotiators are asked why they go to great lengths to avoid being specific about what they want they often say that they do not want the other side to be faced with a 'Yes/No' decision. If they are pressed (as they are at our clinics) they soon reveal that their real inhibition about being specific is the worry that a too early requirement for a decision by the other side could terminate the negotiation because the other side get an opportunity or feel obliged to say 'No'. Let us examine this more closely.

When faced with a specific offer there are two responses we can expect from the other party. Either they say 'Yes' or they say 'No'.

Interestingly, most negotiators fear provoking a 'No'. But if they thought about it at all, they ought to worry most about them saying 'Yes'!

Why? Because, if you get a 'Yes' to your proposition it may be that you have underestimated the strength of your negotiating position. If you offer someone something and expect them to say 'No' and haggle, and instead, they say 'Yes', where does this leave you? Surely a trifle miffed! If they say 'Yes' to your opening offer, what offer should you have opened with? Surely, one that was even better for you than your ideal?

There is nothing more demoralizing to a negotiator than to have his first offer accepted. And this happens a lot more often than you would think. In order to guard against this you need to leave yourself room to 'add-on'.

For example, if you intend to leave yourself room to add-on, your opening offer can be for your basic package: 'My ex-works price is £600 a unit', leaving you scope, if they surprise you and say 'Yes' without attempting to negotiate, to add-on for delivery, special effects, packaging, spares, training, storage, CIF, and so on.

In a variant of add-on ('add-in') you would respond to a 'Yes' to your first offer by qualifying your offer: 'My top price would be £3 million' and then, if they say 'Yes', 'which is for a site cleared and ready for construction', and thus add-in costs for clearing the site, insuring the construction, and

204

securing the fence, with, perhaps, some imaginative proposals for paying the new net sum: 'paid in stages over ten years'.

What if they say 'No' and mean it? Here you would work your offer in the reverse direction by stripping out items that can credibly be dropped without compromising your negotiating position with an obvious revelation that you were trying to rip them off. Hence, you take-off rather than add-on.

If they say 'No' to your demands for £3 million for the site, you can either state that this includes you handing over the site completely clear of debris and properly fenced (if they want more for their money) or the opposite: offer to reduce the price if they will clear the site themselves and be responsible for its security (if their inhibition is the total price of £3 million and they have spare capacity for site clearance).

There are two other possible variations in response to your specific offer. They can say 'Yes' but mean 'No', or say 'No' but mean 'Maybe'.

If they say 'Yes' but mean 'No' you face the problem of eliciting from them exactly what it is that inhibits them from total commitment. In principle they are agreeing with your offer but they have reservations that can develop into a distinct 'No'. Here, you can re-present your offer as a choice that gives them your original offer set against an alternative that takes account of their inhibitions.

You use 'take-off' to adjust your offer and give them a choice. If they say 'Yes' you can choose to 'add-on' (as for a straight 'Yes') or settle; if they say 'No', you have chosen the wrong combination of 'take-offs' and must treat the negotiation here as if it is a straight 'No'. Listening to what they have to say and how they express their reservations on their original 'Yes' is essential if you are to get the revised offer pitched properly.

If they say 'No' but mean 'Maybe' you are in a position to request from them a counter-prosposal. In responding with one they are in effect telling you what the re-presented offer would contain. You can settle (perhaps leaving yourself open to an 'add-on' from them!) or continue to negotiate yourself towards a 'Yes'.

In all cases you can improve your confidence in dealing

with responses to your specific proposals by practising the alternatives of 'add-on' and 'take-off', supported by 'choice' or 'counter-propose'. Being too cautious about being specific drags out the negotiations and indicates a lack of confidence in what you are about.

Our only caveat is that being too specific too early might convince the other side that you have not listened to what they have to say about what they need. But, as in all aspects of negotiating, judgement is a scarce commodity and it separates out the effective negotiators from those who are just average, or worse. A knowledge of tactics, and practice in them, should help you to do better on most occasions than a total lack of awareness that what you think is unique to you and your negotiations, has been, and is being, experienced elsewhere by others, and that tactics are merely a summary of best practice developed painfully over the years. So study them!

Over and under

'Over and under' is a tactic that may be used to block off an unacceptable demand. Just to say 'No' to such demands leaves the other party with the upper hand. The best response is with an 'over and under' counter-proposal. It is designed as a blocking tactic to force the other party to drop their demand by attaching to their demand an unacceptable condition of your own. It is best remembered by the diagram in Figure 7.

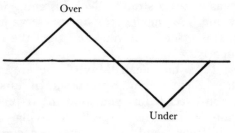

Figure 7

206

The best over and under proposals attach conditions which mirror the other party's demands:

'We require a 75–25 split of the profits.'
'Then we require a 75–25 split of the equity.'

'We demand a 10 per cent settlement discount for payments made within seven days.'
'We would agree to that if you accept a surcharge of 10 per cent on payments received after seven days.'

'We require a penalty clause for orders delivered late.'
'OK, providing we get a premium for all orders that are placed late.'

'We would be happy to pay you a 50 per cent cancellation fee but we must advise you of a reduction in our requirements of 50 per cent next year.'

An over and under is not meant to be accepted and therefore to progress the negotiation it should be followed by a *realistic* conditional proposal.

BID LAST

Airlines sometimes need hotel bedrooms for their passengers if there is an unexpected delay to a flight or a missed connection. When they have a crowd of irate passengers, especially the jet-lagged variety, scrambling around their check-in desks or about to be decanted off the plane they presently occupy, they need swift, sure and certain accommodation available at the end of a single telephone call to a hotel. They cannot suffer the aggravation of looking for a hotel for their passengers when the emergency arises.

Hence, airlines make permanent bookings of hotel rooms at nearby airport hotels. These are held on permanent reservation to the airline; for which the hotel gets a standard payment whether the rooms are occupied or not by the airline's passengers. In return for a guarantee of availability of rooms (which cannot be let to other guests) the hotel receives a guaranteed monthly payment for its unused rooms. The question is what price per room will the airline pay for this service, or, putting it the other way round, what price per room can the hotel expect for rooms which may not be filled anyway if left open for letting?

Airlines negotiate the per room rate individually until they get wiser and contract this out on a collective basis to a single negotiator working for all of them. The result is a heavy pressure on room prices, down in one ruinous year (to the hotels) to one fifth of the normal room charge for other guests.

One hotel chain sought our advice. They complained that when they quoted a price to the airlines' negotiator he took it away and used it to get other chains to offer lower prices (a 'Dutch

(Continued opposite)

auction' gambit) and then came back demanding an even lower rate. How could they stop this ploy?

We suggested that they decide first the rate below which they would prefer to do without the airlines' business (the previous year they had made a large loss on the deal and could have let more rooms).

Next, they should tell the airlines' negotiator that he might as well see the other hotel chains before seeing them as they intended to make only one bid, which they would not in any circumstance amend or repeat for that year, and which he would have to agree to or not there and then.

If he tried to 'Dutch auction' them they would do without the airlines' business for twelve months rather than participate in further negotiations.

The first time they tried this (with much reservation about it as they felt strong pressure to join in the auction rounds) the airlines' negotiator listened to their story, took their price and tried to 'Dutch auction' them again, despite their warnings of the consequences.

They stood firm, however, refused to accept the airlines' pre-booking business for 12 months and filled their hotels with normal guests as best they could and did not suffer below-cost losses on the rooms they let.

The following year the airlines' negotiator got the message. He came to them last. They gave him their price, which had a minute profit margin on it, and he offered them a partial stand-by deal for some of their rooms.

They broke out of the auction, secured some profitable business, and improved their occupancy ratios. The other hotel chains still chase about looking for airlines to give rooms to at less than it costs to service them!

YOU CAN HAVE ANY DEAL YOU WANT AS LONG AS IT'S GREY!

Journalists have a long tradition (without legal basis in Britain) of protecting their sources. They get very emotional about moves to make them reveal who leaked information to them.

Editors do not like to see their staff attacked in this way but neither do they want to involve their paper (and thereby their paper's owners) in damaging legal defences of the asserted rights of staff who refuse to name names. Naturally, staff do not see it that way at all and regard any breach in the 'rule' that their sources are as privileged as a priest's as a dangerous encroachment on the freedom of the press.

In a recent case, an investigative journalist used the services of somebody to tap a person's telephone and record conversations, which, in the journalist's view, provided evidence of crime, though it was a crime itself to bug a telephone in this way (only the Home Secretary is accorded that privilege).

The victim demanded that the courts require the newspaper to reveal the name of the person who had tapped his telephone. The editor at first did not think it worth fighting and was willing to name the tapper, particularly as a refusal could send the journalist to prison for being in contempt of court. Because illegal telephone tapping was involved, he did not believe that the principle at stake was as clear-cut as the usual protection of journalists' sources.

The journalist concerned, and his union, took offence at this interpretation, hired legal counsel, bombarded the editor with protests, and threat-

(Continued opposite)

ened to stop the paper. The journalist was willing to go to jail in defence of his source.

The editor reconsidered his position, reversed his decision to reveal the name of the telephone tapper, and came up with a face-saving statement that caused peace to break out. He said, by way of explanation for his turn around: 'Everything is a variety of a shade of grey. And the journalists persuaded me that this particular shade of grey was different from the one I thought it was!'

Postscript: the court also reached a compromise. It refused the paper the right to print the telephone conversations it had recorded illegally — protecting the victim's legal rights — and refused to order the tapper to be named — protecting the journalist's source.

14 Coping with Deadlock

14.1 Introduction

You win some and you lose some. True. But how many of those negotiations that you lose could be 'saved' if only you had done something different? In this chapter we look at the very real problem of deadlock and answer relevant questions such as: What is the impact of deadlock on the negotiators? How might they cope with it? And how can they overcome deadlock to get agreement even with the most irascible of opponents?

There is no doubt that deadlock is an ever present threat in any negotiation. It can break out at any moment and paralyze the relationship between the parties, sometimes permanently. At best, deadlock will slow down the negotiating process until it is removed; perhaps by a total rethinking of a negotiating position or by the application of sanctions by one or both sides; perhaps by the introduction of some new element into the proposals that mitigates, if not overcomes, the inhibitions that are causing the deadlock.

Fear of deadlock also acts as a damper on the negotiators. It is certainly the largest single cause of inexperienced negotiators making concessions instead of trading them, or of saying 'Yes' too soon when they should have said 'Maybe' (or even 'No').

In industrial relations, deadlock can also be a sought-for outcome by those who prefer strikes to negotiation — the resultant 'fight' and its associated publicity do much more for the 'militant' image than for the interests of the union members.

International relations are not devoid of people who have an interest in deadlock rather than negotiation. An image of militant defence of a country's special interests, be it farm prices, fishing rights, imports, rights of access, mineral rights or whatever, is not reckoned to be contrary to a politician's electoral prospects. It can do wonders for a jaded election campaign, or a bit of domestic unpopularity, to be seen to be standing up to 'foreigners' and attracting the attention of the international media.

An exercise in stage-managed 'deadlock' is fairly common currency in many types of negotiation, including commercial deals. It can arise because the *internal* interests of the other party are served best by the appearance of deadlock. It can arise because making the threat of deadlock real (by apparently deadlocking on an issue) can produce otherwise unobtainable concessions. It can also arise because the parties stumble into deadlock unintentionally and once deadlocked do not know how to get the negotiations moving again.

The last case is of special interest in this chapter, though knowledge of deadlock of the motivated variety is especially important if you have not come across it before (or have not recognized it for what it is when you have experienced it).

14.2   What is deadlock?

Deadlock stops the negotiating process. No further movement is possible unless and until the deadlock is resolved. One or both parties are utterly determined not to make any move on a particular issue and demonstrate their determination by refusing all entreaties other than the surrender of the other party on that issue.

A negotiation can be deadlocked before it begins if an important issue which is not subject to compromise (for whatever reason) dominates all others. If this remains the case then the negotiations will not commence.

An example of this situation is surely the non-negotiations between the Israeli government and the Palestine Liberation

Organization. Apart from the murderous relationship between the two parties (and unless you are involved with one or other side it is difficult to appreciate how each feels about the other as a result of years of mutual 'atrocities'), there is an apparently unbridgeable gulf between them on the issue of recognition or not of the state of Israel. The PLO withholds recognition of Israel until its claims for territory are settled (and some Palestinians appear willing to continue their non-recognition policy even if it means that their territorial claims are never conceded by Israel); meanwhile, Israel withholds recognition of the PLO as the 'sole and legitimate representative of the Palestinian people' and refuses to negotiate anything with them until the PLO recognizes Israel's right to exist (and some Israelis appear willing never to concede recognition of the PLO even if this means permanent unrest and the risk of war over its borders).

Negotiations can deadlock over an issue that emerges as being not subject to movement by one or both sides. Negotiations over the introduction of new technology in the printing industry were deadlocked for years over the introduction of new technology and over a subsidiary issue, the union membership of the employees who operate the new technology.

For example, with current technology (it's been around for some years now) it does not require a skilled 'hot-metal' typesetter to prepare manuscripts for printing. Anybody trained in keyboard skills can do the job adequately — indeed, journalists can enter their copy for a newspaper direct to the sub-editors in a form that is ready for paste-up without the intermediary help of a traditional typesetter. Negotiations to introduce technology were deadlocked on the issue of whose fingers are to touch-type on the keyboard; those of the highly skilled but now obsolete typesetters or those of journalists, skilled typists and retrained anybodies?

The deadlock was broken by the entry of non-union printers into the industry, and the determination by existing managers not to continue the old ways of producing newspapers. After some hard fought disputes, the unions decided to drop their opposition and negotiate a compromise.

The most common form of deadlock is, of course, the firm

statement of the word 'No'. Fear of hearing 'No' compels many sales people to go to great lengths to elicit a 'Yes', largely by making all kinds of pre-emptive concessions in the face of the buyer's stony silence. Experience of sales people and their practice of making concessions when faced with a buyer's apparent hostility and indifference teaches buyers to act in the way that gets them the most concessions. Because they frequently act in this way, many sellers think that this is the true nature of buyers and thus the fear of deadlock perpetuates itself by provoking them into 'yes' seeking behaviour. The circle is as vicious as it is unnecessary.

Deadlock can degenerate into outright hostilities and, in the extreme, the parties can try and kill each other. The 'offer you cannot refuse' can become so because the alternative is to have your brains blown out. More frequently (unless you trade with people made famous by the film *The Godfather*!) the hostilities that arise from deadlock can mean a total breach in the commercial, industrial, international or domestic relationship of the parties.

Not a few former clients refuse to have any dealings with each other (and encourage others to do likewise by gossip and innuendo). The exact cause of the breakdown in any particular case could be a single event (a refusal to alter the agreed terms of payment for example) or a series of events (overdue accounts, missed deliveries, frequent bickering over details, refusals to concede changes across a whole range of items, and just a general lack of trust).

Deadlock has a price. Its most obvious first price is the fact that the time spent in trying to negotiate a deal is wasted. Time wasted in one negotiation prohibits time being spent productively in another.

If the negotiation is a long one, such as a major contract with a foreign government, especially a long-winded communist government, the time wasted through deadlock is not a small cost to the losers. In fact, the very fact of the long time spent in getting to the point of deadlock has been known to push some companies into accepting terms which otherwise they would reject on commercial grounds, in order to salvage something (the Russians do this a lot, and why shouldn't they if they find that Western firms crumble when faced with the threat of deadlock!).

The next obvious price is the cost of not getting a settlement or agreement. The costs here are of two kinds: the long-term financial costs to both sides because each misses out on a profitable relationship; and the immediate costs of having to endure a period of mutually imposed sanctions such as strikes, lock-outs, embargoes and wars.

14.3 Fear of deadlock

The best advice we can give to those negotiators who worry about facing deadlock is: RELAX! Far too many negotiators are intimidated by the prospect of deadlock. They give it altogether too great an importance and allow it to structure their behaviour before they even know what the other side wants or how badly they want it.

If you work for a firm that has 20 per cent of the market for the products it sells (if you don't know your company's market share you ought not to be working for them), this means that one in five potential buyers are purchasing your company's products. Now, being realistic, you are unlikely to be winning deals with 100 per cent of your prospects in this situation, in the short run. Hence, you are going to face deadlock, on average, four times out of five. You will get four 'Nos' to every 'Yes'.

True, you can become a super-duper sales negotiator and score five out of five, or at least that is what your sales manager will try to tell you (he has to, that is his job). But in the real world, if you think about it, you are unlikely to reverse market trends in your territory overnight and raise your company's market share much above 20 per cent, if that is where it is when you start.

Hence, select a lower achievement level than the fantasies of the sales manager. If your market share is 20 per cent, then your minimum achievement level is 20 per cent. So relax. Be ready for four deadlocks out of five. If you do, you will gradually find that you will increase your score from 20 per cent towards 30 per cent, though not in one go.

If you are ready for deadlock, instead of fearing it, you will relax and become more confident in your negotiating. Confidence in your presentations will breed confidence in your handling of proposals, in your handling of bargaining language (IF . . . THEN), and in your willingness to say 'No' to propositions that make you and your company worse off.

If you are tense with worry about getting a 'No', it will show in all your contact with the other party. Your use of the argument step will be fraught with panic-stricken efforts to avoid offending the other side. Once they get your measure in argument they will get confidence to massage you with their proposals and finally finish you off with impudent conditional bargaining.

Instead of a profitable agreement (that gives you a commission!) you might get an order on, or even below, your company's bottom line (which puts you on basic salary and the sales manager's interview list) or, more likely, you won't even get the order as they prefer to deal with companies that have more faith in their products by sending out people to sell them who have more confidence in themselves than you seem to display.

If there is any single cause of unconditional offers, especially of the 'free gift' variety aimed at creating 'goodwill' in the other party, it lies in the fear of deadlock. Some negotiators wrongly believe that deadlock occurs because the other side does not 'like' them enough, or that the buyers 'like' their rivals better. Nothing could be more misleading than to think that deadlock will be avoided if you start conceding in search of goodwill or crawling in search of friendship.

Put the prospect of deadlock in perspective. You cannot win them all, unless you have a monopoly, but if you are a monopolist you need not bother too much about negotiating!

Much the same is true of industrial relations. If you indicate, intentionally or otherwise, that you wish at all costs to avoid deadlock, then it will not be long before the other side learn to hint at the prospect of deadlock in order to force concessions.

It is well known that inexperienced union negotiators introduce the prospect of sanctions (strikes, etc.) very early on in the negotiations and repeat themselves on this theme many times during the sessions. With them it's always a case of 'or else', either explicitly or implicitly. Inexperienced managements will react to these threats, either by crumbling or, just as bad, by retaliatory bluster in kind, when their best course of action is to compare the credibility of the threat with their own judgement as to the likelihood of it being carried out (based, of course, on your thorough preparation). Certainly, they should not be intimidated by the fear of deadlock. They should relax more, and worry less, and get on with the negotiation as an exercise in trading not conceding.

Relax and you will get them to settle for less!

14.4   Avoid provocation

Deadlocks are real. They occur in many negotiations despite the best efforts of the negotiators. Some of these deadlocks are purely temporary, others can be permanent.

Why do deadlocks occur? The simple answer is that people cause deadlocks. They have interests, inhibitions, fears, likes and dislikes, prejudices, opinions, ambitions, guilts and consciences, good and bad manners, hopes, attitudes and wide-ranging behaviours. These are woven through the issues in dispute and they mould the response to the potential compromises that might produce a settlement.

The fact that a negotiation is taking place at all is itself a great step towards a mutually agreed settlement, and this ought not to be underestimated. Negotiation is only one method of settling a dispute. The parties could have chosen one or more alternatives to negotiation: they could have sought legal redress, passive or violent demonstration, boycott, arbitration, strike, go-slow, occupation, appeals to the public conscience, legislation, and so on. But if they are negotiating they have foregone (at least for the moment) any or all of these alternatives.

Once parties agree to negotiate they enter a unique process that normally eschews open conflict as a means of bringing about a settlement. (Though not always — while many industrial relations negotiations take place with the management insisting that it is not 'under duress' by strike action, sometimes it is unavoidable, and likewise internationally, where the best that can be obtained is a ceasefire.) For a start then, a requirement that both parties negotiate in good faith is often a trifle idealistic but, to the extent that the ambience of the negotiations implies good faith, it is more likely that deadlock will be avoided, or sooner overcome if it materializes.

For this reason it is good advice when negotiating with a party on an issue that is likely to lead to deadlock, because the ideal positions of both sides are extremely far apart and the likelihood of there being an early identification of an overlap is remote, not to do anything that is likely to exacerbate charges of bad faith by the other side. In other words, do not provoke them with provocative behaviour, or, more precisely, with what they are likely to regard as provocative behaviour.

Actions of a provocative nature can be avoided while the issue is being settled by negotiation. The *status quo*, or the *status quo ante*, can be maintained, though which of these will be agreed to will depend a great deal on the balance of power between the parties. If a commercial dispute arises, say over rights to a product design, it may not be conducive to a settlement if the party accused of piracy continues to publicize its setting up of a distribution network to sell the disputed product while negotiations are in progress.

What constitutes a provocation is decided by the parties concerned. If they disagree over a particular action it might strain the negotiations to breaking point, or provoke some other response. Ceasefire agreements in a war often break down over what one side perceives as a breach by the other side (Lebanon has for long been a classic case of war being an activity between ceasefires).

The best source for what the other side perceives is, of course, themselves, and a careful study of the other side's positions on the contentious issues should provide sufficient clues as to how they are likely to perceive your actions. But if you are still in doubt, ask them!

If you must take specific actions in areas that might possibly lead to deadlock, then you should be as open about your intentions and the limitations of what you propose as you can. If a building tenancy is in dispute, you ought to carefully

PROVOCATIVE BEHAVIOUR PROVOKES

Whenever tempers cool in the Middle East, extremists on one or other side go to great lengths to stir things up again. The shooting of moderate PLO leaders by unknown assassins has the effect of shifting the remaining leadership from considering accommodation with Israel to continuing outright opposition.

The Israeli government has been known to embark on much publicized new settlement policies on the West Bank whenever it looked like the Arabs were moving towards accepting some sort of deal that gave them autonomy without sovereignty. The resultant new settlements inflamed Arab opinion and made it impossible for the PLO to make compromises.

There is some, scanty and controversial, evidence that the Japanese military authorized the attack on Pearl Harbour in 1941 without the authority of the government in order to prevent a negotiated settlement to emerge between the Japanese and US governments.

More recently, much speculation has been raised by the timing of the British sinking of the Argentinian warship, the *Belgrano*, and the presentation of Peru's peace proposals to end the occupation of the Falklands by Argentina. Critics argue that Prime Minister Thatcher deliberately ordered the sinking of the *Belgrano* in order to force the Argentinians to oppose the Peruvian peace plan and thus enable her to settle the dispute by force of arms. (The evidence supporting this allegation, it should be noted, is highly selective and by no means clearcut and much of it to date (1986) supports a different, more innocent, interpretation.)

inform the other side why you are changing the locks (security, lost keys, contract maintenance, etc.) or removing the roof (necessary repairs, etc.). Otherwise they might conclude that you are about to abandon the negotiations for some other solution.

14.5 Public commitment

Disputes are news. You have to face that fact and allow for it in your negotiating behaviour. The more you are in the public eye, however, the more difficult it will be to reach a settlement.

Deadlock is more likely where each side has gone public on its ideal, especially if they have accompanied their public stance with firm, unyielding rhetoric in which they have advertised their willingness to go to hell and back before they surrender an inch.

Trade union leaders, politicians and soon-to-be-divorced couples have a strong proclivity for public stances. The union leaders talk to their members and the general public and hope that by making a public stance the other side will be intimidated into believing that they prefer a bitter dispute to losing face. Politicians always go public and hope that this intimidates other politicians (and other governments) into realizing just how serious they are about their ideal. Couples, of course, try to line up the family on their side and make life miserable for those who stay neutral or join the opposing camp.

Going public is almost always bad news. It makes it difficult to reach a negotiated settlement because a strong public stance on an ideal precludes an early movement towards a limit position. In negotiating, the opening stance is not the one we expect realistically to end up with and the more public we make our opening stance the less easy it is to move at all, and if we do not move we have deadlock.

Even in the negotiating process itself too strong a commitment to an opening position, continued for too long, will provoke deadlock if the other side become convinced that you are not prepared to move at all. You know what to do about this from reading earlier chapters on the eight steps.

14.6 Don't make things worse

If the other side does not trust you, it does not help your case to rake over the past by asking them *why* they lack trust in you. Asking why is the weakest thing you can do, especially when they have rehearsed their reasons in earlier sessions or occasions. To move away from deadlock you have to get the argument away from the *why* questions to the *how* questions: How can we avoid lack of trust in future? How can we ensure that what you have complained about does not happen again? How can we meet your minimum requirements for continuing to do business with us? How can we ensure that you do not feel threatened by the new arrangements? — and so on.

If you concentrate on *why*, you will get told and in the telling they might start off a round of mutual blame and recriminations that further cement the deadlock rather than unblock it. Only a special breed of negotiators can sit and listen impassively to a tirade of illegitimate abuse about their failings and even a saint can be driven to feel an urge to defend his actions when attacked quite wrongly for something he neither did nor ever intended to do.

If deadlock occurs at the argument stage you should know now what not to do: above all break out of the argument with a positive proposal of some kind, and the *how* question is one such way to do so.

We do not suggest that this is easy (if it was you would not be worth what your employers are, or ought to be, paying you). The high tension associated with a deadlock is bound to pile emotional pressure on you and your opponent. The argument step is always the one associated with the deadlock, for if you are not arguing you are unlikely to be in deadlock! If you display lack of respect, trust and belief in them and their statements, you are likely to stay in deadlock, or worse, exacerbate it.

Hence, questions that are loaded ('Do you believe you are always right?'), impertinent ('How long are you going to

222

waffle for?'), Perry Mason ('Why do you claim to be innocent when you admit liability?'), boomerang type ('Don't you agree that you made a cock-up once again?), or 'gotcha' type ('Wouldn't you do anything to save your reputation?') are self-defeating. They worsen the deadlock.

Make things happen for you by asking open-type questions. Search for questions that require more than one word in the answer ('Yes', 'No', 'Never' etc.). Ask a question to get the other party to respond and talk through their perceptions and views — the longer they take with their answers the lower the hostility level will become, providing, of course, that you do not interrupt them or start attacking them (even non-verbally by shaking your head, or looking angry, or obviously not listening).

14.7   Finding an agenda

British diplomats of the old school developed a useful device for defusing deadlock which is now fairly common throughout the world. This was the 'headings' approach. Faced with two sides in bitter confrontation and total deadlock, they sought to move the initial negotiations away from the details of the issues in dispute to the potential headings for future discussion in the form of an agenda.

The parties did not have to agree at all on what they disagreed about. All they had to do was to agree to discuss the issues according to an agenda. Once the parties agreed to the list of headings for discussion the proper atmosphere was created for negotiations to proceed.

The first step towards ending the deadlock is taken by each side agreeing to a common agenda. There might very well be problems with the parties as to the order of items on the agenda, as well as to the list of items itself. One side may wish an item to be given priority, the other side might wish another. One side wants to include something that the other side wishes to exclude. In the British–Argentinian negotiations, the issue of whether sovereignty over the Falklands is an appropriate agenda item has to be handled before any negotiations can take place. Until a formula is found nothing can proceed.

If the parties agree that an agenda is possible and, having found one that is mutually satisfactory, if they agree that the agenda can form the basis for a negotiation, they are on their way to tackling the deadlock. For if they answer 'Yes' to the question 'Can we proceed in this way' they are effectively saying that they wish to proceed in that way.

14.8   Effective questions

Questions, we have said several times, are a most useful negotiating tool. They are also grossly neglected by average and poor negotiators. The effective negotiator spends a lot more time asking questions and *listening carefully to the answers.*

Parties in deadlock need a safe-conduct pass to move from their ideal positions. They will resist being forced or pressurised into abandoning the relative safety of their opening positions. To persuade them to move at all requires their permission (the obverse of their veto).

By asking them to agree to an agenda in a form that asks 'Could/would/should we work to this agenda' you are effectively asking them for their permission. If they wish to withhold their permission for any reason, then you have to return to the negotiation on the agenda. It might take time but there is no other way if you wish to negotiate a settlement. You can ask them what suggestions they have for improving the agenda or for a statement of their views. Either way you should listen to their replies and decide whether to incorporate them in a revised agenda.

If they agree to work to the agenda you can use more questions to move the negotiations along. If they are claiming damages from you for something they allege that you did, instead of arguing the toss about their right to damages, and without prejudice to whether you accept that right at all, you could ask them 'What damages are you seeking?'

In effect you are trying to move them from the grievance they feel they have towards the remedy that they are proposing. If they have not got a remedy in mind yet, you can get them to specify how they quantify their losses: 'How many hours did you actually lose in down-time because our spares were not available?', 'When specifically did our supplies cease arriving at the site?', 'What have you included in your estimates of refabrication costs for the defective items?', and so on.

In general, no claim for damages (for example) is ever a minor one, as no engineer ever believes that a failing on a supplier's part ever caused minimal disruption to his project (similarly, no sales negotiator ever thinks a requirement to return to the office for a meeting with the sales manager costs a small sale — sales negotiators only lose big sales if somebody else is to 'blame'). By looking closer at the other party's claims you might get them more into perspective. So might they.

By testing the feelings of the other party about potential solutions to the dispute you open up possibilities for making tentative proposals: 'How do you feel about the use of part-time labour?', 'Is it possible to relax the reporting require-ments in this sort of situation?', 'Have you any views on the use of non-union labour?', 'How would your people react to random vehicle searches?' etc.

The answers may not always be positive (they have a right to their veto) but they may be illustrative of their real position. The more they tell you about their feelings the more they expose the options that might settle the dispute. The mere fact that you are clearly searching for solutions could be instrumental in breaking the deadlock. Their perception may have been that you had a one-track mind in the negotiations and intended to impose on them a single solution that was totally unsatisfactory. By showing them otherwise you unravel the deadlock.

14.9   Search for criteria

If genuine deadlock is to be unravelled, then genuine criteria must be found for doing so. Criteria separate the subjective pressures on the negotiators from more or less objective tests of the proposed solutions.

225

Unions sometimes insist on comparability (especially if their members compare unfavourably with their named comparable occupations — be sure they will always choose occupations with higher pay than their members), and sometimes they insist on other criteria such as productivity or profitability. If they can force the issue with their brute strength they may not even mention any other criteria than 'Give us what we want, or else!'

Criteria are, however, a better guide to a settlement than the alternative of brute strength and ignorance. Finding suitable criteria is itself a negotiation! Each party will try to introduce the criteria most favourable to its own case. The well prepared party will have searched through various criteria to select the set that suits them most. The other party had better make sure that it has searched similarly through the available criteria and considered them thoroughly too. Botched arithmetic in preparation will tumble down around you once it is exposed to the other side.

This is the purpose of the search for appropriate criteria. If the parties agree on a set of criteria (perhaps because there are 'swings and roundabouts' in the proposed set), they automatically separate the eventual solution to the dispute from the relative strength of the parties. Even in a ceasefire negotiation, by selecting an imminent date or time for the ceasefire to take effect they preclude a major shift in territorial gains and losses by either side which might otherwise jeopardise the prospects of a ceasefire. Thus, an agreement to a ceasefire with each side 'holding the territory it has at 11 a.m. tomorrow' is hardly likely to result in anything other than marginal changes in the front line — especially as the troops may not be motivated to strive very hard to capture territory at real risk of their lives if they know there is to be a ceasefire within a few hours.

The decision on criteria enables the negotiating process to go on to fill in the details that are applied to the criteria. If comparability is decided upon, the parties must decide with what or whom comparisons are to be made; differential treatment for different cases requires deciding on how much differential treatment for which different/similar cases; equitable treatment requires specification of how equitable the treat-

226

ment must be; fair and reasonable requires definitions of how fair and how reasonable if it is to be applied, and so on.

The criteria themselves are negotiable. Their application will be subject to scrutiny by each side and judgements made as to whether they constitute an appropriate settlement of the dispute. Parties can and do revise their attitude to continuing with a search for a negotiated settlement. At some point they may decide that they prefer deadlock to negotiating, and in such circumstance you will have to go through the entire process again. Of course, this may not be an attractive option and you might have to revise your own attitude to seeking a negotiated settlement instead of trying something else, or decide to abandon the issue altogether.

There is no doubt that finding a negotiated solution requires patience and, bearing in mind that there may not be an alternative to living with deadlock for some considerable period, you do not always have the option for a solution by negotiation set neatly against a solution by some other means.

14.10 Use your imagination

Finally, an additional plea for you to think creatively when faced with deadlock. Your opponents may be disagreeing with you because the form in which you have presented your proposals includes some item totally at variance with their basic inhibitions. Perhaps both sides have got bogged down in a far too narrow approach to the dispute? If so, the answer is to seek out new versions of the proposals — to re-package them in some way.

Thinking creatively about the tradable variables introduces new elements into the deal. You do not know what is going on in the heads of your opponents. When they say 'No' they might just be trying to test your resolve — and why shouldn't they do so if experience teaches them that it pays to be firm?

All deals involve variables, though some are more obvious than others. If your present proposals have resulted in deadlock, then you should look at the package and review what they have said to you in the negotiations. Have they indicated something significant about your proposals that you ought to

227

reconsider? If you have been listening you will have received signals about their inhibitions.

Can you change the way the money is presented? How do they pay, in which currency, on what credit terms, with what discounts for cash, in advance, in arrears, cash on delivery or on approval? How regularly should they pay instalments? To whom do they pay? Who gets the interest on cash lying in the accounts? What are the consequences for default? and so on?

Can you alter the delivery arrangements: Who delivers? Who collects? In what quantities? Who pays the insurance and freight? Who covers loss and damage? Who inspects for the same? How is it to be packaged? Is it sale-or-return? What minimum loads are possible? Can we break bulk and, if so, where? Who pays storage? How regularly can we document movements? What quantities can be re-ordered? What response time is needed for re-orders? and so on?

What about the specifications? Engineers *always* over-specify because they like to get the latest equipment with the most up-to-date features. They also like to cover themselves just in case something goes wrong. If you do not believe this, compare a company whose spares are ordered by their engineers with one whose spares are ordered by their accountants!

Hence, can we alter the specifications in some way to lower costs or improve the package? Which are the critical specifications on an item? Can they be varied in any way or met by some other means? Just how reliable do we want our equipment to be, given the existence of instant response by maintenance engineers? Is a doubled working life for equipment worth a treble or quadruple price? If we halve the specifications how much do we save? Should some extras be standard and some standards be extras? Just how many of these attractive features are actually used?

This last is very obvious when pointed out. For instance, take a close look at the pocket calculator that you use and ask yourself just how many of the functions it is capable of you actually use regularly? We suspect, largely from our own experience and observation, that you use far fewer of the available functions than you have paid for (and don't think

228

this applies only to industrial products: take a look at the kitchen oven with its automatic timers, or your video with its audio dubbing and recording capabilities. Be honest: when did you last use them? How ever long that was, remember that you paid for them!).

Time is, of course, the big variable. It breaks more dead-locks than almost all the rest put together. Time is divisible and, being divisible, it is eminently suitable to break a dead-lock. Alter when the agreement starts, or when bits of it start, and you unlock a deadlock.

If something is being proposed that the other side is deadly suspicious of, introduce a time variable that permits a review of the situation at some date in the future and you might have done enough to save the other side's face or reassure them in some way.

You can use time to specify who gets something (length of service?), when they get it (from 1988), for how long (until they retire) and when others might qualify for it (1990).

You can use time to state when payments are to be made (after delivery, during construction), and how frequently (every month, quarter, annually). You can use time to specify when reports are to be made, complaints to be heard, issues

---

DEADLOCK COSTS

A cold storage manager had a dispute with an engineering supplier over a particular invoice. He adopted the stance that the supplier would receive no more business until he modified the bill. The supplier refused and the cold store stopped giving him any more business.

The cold storage manager admits to great difficulty in finding alternative suppliers whose work is as good as his previous supplier or who are as prompt on service calls. He is unable to find a face-saving formula which will allow him to re-open negotiations with his former supplier without appearing to be giving in.

---

to be settled, and work to be completed. It is infinitely variable and the most useful negotiator's tool when faced with deadlock.

These are just some of the ways of looking at tradable variables. Each business has its own variables and it is worth your while to take a new look at your business and its products and list all the variables you can think of that might apply to them.

DO WE REALLY NEED THIS?

In business, the amount of machinery that is purchased that is way above the actual requirements of the process would probably surprise you (and would certainly interest your accountants). If you can alter the specification you might break the deadlock.

For example, in a recent major purchase of an office automation system the negotiators were very worried at the size of the annual maintenance charge that was looming on the equipment. By asking the seller why they charged so much (15 per cent of the capital cost per year) they discovered that this was to provide an instant three-hour response if there was a breakdown in any item. But with the size and extent of this major purchase, and with much of the equipment available in quadruple cover, it did not seem necessary to pay for such an early response.

By re-designing the maintenance cover to confine the instant maintenance response to a breakdown in the mainframe only and to allow up to 48 hours for ancillary items and workstations to be repaired, the maintenance charge was reduced to under 3 per cent, well within the purchaser's budget (they bought some extra micros on the money they saved, which pleased the sales negotiator too).

Be ready for some surprises. It is so very easy to get into a narrow rut with a product you have been selling or buying for years, and for the number of variables actually negotiated about to be reduced to one or two, when there may be dozens available that you have forgotten about through non-use.

Basically, therefore, deadlock is a feature of the negotiating process. If you are worried by it you are more likely to experience it. If you can cope with it, by having confidence, asking the right questions, applying your imagination to the variables applicable to the deal then you are more likely to win some and lose fewer than if you don't.

14.11 Checklist for coping with deadlock

- Relax and sell more.
- Relax and make them settle for less.
- Avoid provocation.

- Going public invites deadlock.
- Ask *how* questions rather than *why*.
- *Listen* to the answers.
- Agree on an agenda.
- Establish criteria for settling issues.
- Use your imagination by using variables.

14.12 Common avoidable mistakes

- Being over-anxious to get agreement
- Having unrealistic goals
- Behaving in a provocative manner
- Trying to coerce the other party with your public statements
- Asking loaded questions
- Not asking open questions
- Not questioning the basis on which both sides have decided their proposals
- Not establishing sound criteria
- Not considering all the tradable variables

15 Conclusions

We end where we began: negotiations are a part of everyday life. You will now be better equipped having worked your way through the book at least to understand what is going on in those negotiations you play a part in. Improving your performance will take a little extra time and effort. Reading about a skill is not the same as practising it. But you have made the start by reading about it. You must now set yourself the definite and measurable objective of practising the negotiating skills we have written about.

You will make the most improvement fastest by copying out the checklists of the eight steps and the lists of common avoidable mistakes. Writing is a great aid to memory jogging later on when you are making your moves.

If we were asked to state the rock bottom guide to negotiating for someone motivated to learn we would emphasize the four main phases of negotiation (PREPARE, ARGUE, PROPOSE, BARGAIN) and put it thus: Prepare by knowing your business, Listen to the argument, Make conditional proposals, Bargain using IF . . . THEN. If you work to that format right away and build on it as your confidence grows, you will get better deals than you normally get, and you will get some deals where you normally deadlock.

There is no mystery about negotiating. It is not a game that only the devious can play (we doubt very much whether the devious are any good at negotiating at all). Negotiating is a skill that can be learned and improved on by almost anybody. Using the Eight-step Approach you can analyze your own performance. You can also analyze the negotiations that are going on around you in the world. Observation can also be of great help in your own learning.

Watching what the world's 'experts' do in their negotiations is a very sobering experience, especially if you believe that they are better negotiators than you are just because they claim to be experts. When you analyze what they are doing, using the Eight-step Approach, you will be amazed how much better you feel about your own performance! But do not get carried away with your ego: at every football match that is ever played there are many more people watching who believe they are better than the 22 'idiots' chasing the ball on the field; at least that is what one must conclude listening to the crowd's comments.

Use your daily newspaper to follow the major negotiations in industry and world affairs. If the negotiation interests you cut out the stories and keep a file. Read into the background of the negotiations using your local library (or rather, in the interests of authors everywhere, visit your bookshop and buy a book).

Keep a note of some of the memorable phrases you will hear in any negotiation. If they are really effective on you, practise using them. Look out for the howlers too. By amusing you they will also teach you. The best mistakes to learn by are the ones you can correct most easily: your own. So be self-critical occasionally.

Above all else remember: all your propositions must always be led by your conditions. IF YOU remember that THEN you will get better bargains, everytime. IF you don't, you won't. It's as simple as that.

Suggestions for Further Reading

The literature on negotiating is extensive and expanding. Much of it is of a highly academic nature and mostly inaccessible to the general reader. We have selected a few contributions to the study of negotiating which may be of interest to those readers whose appetites have been whetted by reading this book.

Most good libraries stock Richard E. Walton and Robert B. McKersie: *A Behavioural Theory of Labor Negotiations: an analysis of a social interaction system*, McGraw-Hill, New York, 1965. This is an eminently readable book whatever impression the title may otherwise give you. It illustrates its points by using examples from live negotiations in the American labour market. Walton and McKersie have had an enormous influence on the study of negotiating. In this book we have used the concept of the negotiating continuum which made its original appearance in the literature in Walton and McKersie's *distributional bargaining model*. The book concludes with a bibliography of 200 items.

William Zartman edited another American book on negotiating: *The 50% Solution: how to bargain successfully with hijackers, strikers, bosses, oil magnates, Arabs, Russians, and other worthy opponents in this modern world*, Anchor Books, Doubleday, New York, 1976. As with the previous book the title is misleading; this is a collection of serious essays on negotiations carefully selected by the editor who lectures in Negotiation and Diplomacy at New York University. It is the kind of book you can dip into and return to time and again. There are thirteen detailed case studies and eight more general evaluations. The book ends with a bibliography of over 300 titles covering the whole field of negotiating.

Thomas C. Schelling, *The Strategy of Conflict*, Harvard University Press, Cambridge, Mass., 1960, is the classic (but difficult) text on international negotiation; Roger Fisher, *International Conflict for Beginners*, Harper and Row, New York, 1969, is both readable and perceptive.

Several recent books on negotiating can be consulted. The first by Roger Fisher and William Ury: *Getting to YES: negotiating agreement without giving in*, Hutchinson, 1983, has many brilliant insights into structuring your approach to negotiating. Fisher and Ury have made an impact on negotiating practice with their advice to shift the dispute from positions to principles, to separate the people from the problem and develop the Best Alternative to a Negotiated Agreement (BATNA) as a test of your options.

Howard Raiffa's *The Art and Science of Negotiation*, Harvard University, 1982, makes accessible to non-mathematical readers much of the interesting work in applying decision analysis to negotiating problems. The cases used to illustrate his message are extremely valuable. For an application of this approach to the construction business see P. V. D. Marsh's *Contract Negotiation Handbook*, Gower, Aldershot, 1984.

One of the authors of this book: Gavin Kennedy, has written *Everything is Negotiable!*, Business Books, 1983, which covers the entire spectrum of business negotiation and includes nineteen sets of self-assessment questions on which to try out your negotiating skills. This was followed in 1985 by *Negotiate Anywhere: doing business abroad*, Hutchinson Business, and in 1986 by *Superdeal: how to negotiate anything*, also published by Hutchinson Business.

Readers interested in keeping abreast of recent developments in negotiating writing should subscribe to *Negotiation Journal*, available from Harvard Law School, 500 Pound Lane, Cambridge, Massachusetts 02138, USA.

Index